Study Skills for Master's Level Students

A Reflective Approach for Health and Social Care

Health and Social Care titles from Lantern Publishing Ltd

Clinical Skills for Student Nurses edited by Robin Richardson
ISBN 978 1 906052 04 1

Understanding Research and Evidence-based Practice by Bruce Lindsay
ISBN 978 1 906052 01 0

Values for Care Practice by Sue Cuthbert and Jan Quallington
ISBN 978 1 906052 05 8

Communication and Interpersonal Skills by Elaine Donnelly and Lindsey Neville
ISBN 978 1 906052 06 5

Numeracy, Clinical Calculations and Basic Statistics by Neil Davison
ISBN 978 1 906052 07 2

Essential Study Skills edited by Marjorie Lloyd and Peggy Murphy
ISBN 978 1 906052 14 0

Safe and Clean Care by Tina Tilmouth with Simon Tilmouth
ISBN 978 1 906052 08 9

Neonatal Care edited by Amanda Williamson and Kenda Crozier
ISBN 978 1 906052 09 6

Fundamentals of Diagnostic Imaging edited by Anne-Marie Dixon
ISBN 978 1 906052 10 2

Fundamentals of Nursing Care by Anne Llewellyn and Sally Hayes
ISBN 978 1 906052 13 3

The Care and Wellbeing of Older People edited by Angela Kydd, Tim Duffy and F.J. Raymond Duffy
ISBN 978 1 906052 15 7

Palliative Care edited by Elaine Stevens and Janette Edwards
ISBN 978 1 906052 16 4

Interpersonal Skills for the People Professions edited by Lindsey Neville
ISBN 978 1 906052 18 8

Understanding and Helping People in Crisis by Elaine Donnelly, Briony Williams and Tess Parkinson
ISBN 978 1 906052 21 8

A Handbook for Student Nurses by Wendy Benbow and Gill Jordan (second edition 2013)
ISBN 978 1 908625 14 4

Professional Practice in Public Health edited by Jill Stewart and Yvonne Cornish
ISBN 978 1 906052 20 1

The Care Process by Sally Hayes and Anne Llewellyn
ISBN 978 1 906052 22 5

Genetics by Karen Vipond (revised edition 2013)
ISBN 978 1 908625 15 1

Understanding Wellbeing edited by Anneyce Knight and Allan McNaught
ISBN 978 1 908625 00 7

Developing Reflective Practice by Natius Oelofsen
ISBN 978 1 908625 01 4

Leadership in Health and Social Care by Louise Jones and Clare L. Bennett
ISBN 978 1 908625 02 1

REVISED EDITION

Study Skills for Master's Level Students

A Reflective Approach for Health and Social Care

Debbie Casey, Liz Clark and Sally Hayes

Lantern

ISBN: 978 1 908625 17 5
Revised edition published in 2013 by Lantern Publishing Limited

First edition (ISBN 978 1 906052 26 3) published in 2011 by Reflect Press Limited

Lantern Publishing Limited, The Old Hayloft, Vantage Business Park, Bloxham Rd, Banbury OX16 9UX, UK

www.lanternpublishing.com

British Library Cataloguing in Publication Data
A catalogue record for this book is available from the British Library

The authors and publisher have made every attempt to ensure the content of this book is up to date and accurate. However, healthcare knowledge and information is changing all the time so the reader is advised to double-check any information in this text on drug usage, treatment procedures, the use of equipment, etc. to confirm that it complies with the latest safety recommendations, standards of practice and legislation, as well as local Trust policies and procedures. Students are advised to check with their tutor and/or mentor before carrying out any of the procedures in this textbook.

Typeset by Medlar Publishing Solutions, India
Cover design by Andrew Magee Design Ltd
Printed and bound by MPG Books Ltd, Bodmin, UK
Distributed by NBN International, 10 Thornbury Rd, Plymouth PL6 7PP, UK

CONTENTS

This book is dedicated to all the health and social care students who have inspired and motivated us in our teaching. We hope the book will enable future students to aim high and achieve their potential in their studies.

ABBREVIATIONS

AACN	American Association of Colleges of Nursing
AP	Advanced Practitioner
CASP	Critical Appraisal Skills Programme
CATS	Credit Accumulation and Transfer Scheme
CPD	Continuing Professional Development
DH	Department of Health
FHEQ	The Framework for Higher Education Qualifications
HCPC	Health and Care Professions Council
HE	Higher Education
HEI	Higher Education Institute
ICMJ	International Committee of Medical Journal Editors
IT	Information Technology
NHSI	National Health Service Institute for Innovation
NICE	National Institute for Health and Clinical Excellence
NMC	Nursing and Midwifery Council
PhD	Doctor of Philosophy
QAA	Quality Assurance Agency for Higher Education
RCT	Randomised Controlled Trial
REF	Research Excellence Framework
SQ3R	Survey, Question, Read, etc.
SWOT	Strengths, Weaknesses, Opportunities and Threats
VLE	Virtual Learning Environment

INTRODUCTION

In the current context of an increasing graduate workforce and the resulting development of postgraduate provision for continuing professional development (CPD), there is a general understanding in higher education (HE) circles that, at postgraduate level, students aim to be independent and self-directed learners. Therefore, within Master's level courses there exists an expectation of relative independence alongside an emphasis on the centrality of the student's individual learning needs. As experienced senior lecturers working in HE, we feel that there is a paucity of guidance to enable students to understand what becoming an 'independent learner' entails and on how to identify and recognise individual learning needs.

This text will therefore explore the world of Master's study – its context, regulation and operation – in order to assist students to develop capability in both thinking and writing at Master's level. This will be achieved through the use of practical and reflective activities aimed at recognising and developing the use of higher academic skills. Such skills include critical thinking, using literature and writing to demonstrate distinctive and independent thought with the synthesis of ideas and critical engagement with alternative views. Also, through being encouraged to think reflectively, analytical thinking skills and self-learning will be developed.

However, please note that this text will focus mainly on the needs of taught Master's students (for our definition of what this is, please see Chapter 1). Also note that, although research as a discipline is not specifically addressed in the text, the thinking and writing skills required for undertaking a research project are developed throughout the book. Research skills will be referred to in the text and the students will be signposted to the plethora of texts that exist specifically to develop skills in research methods.

USING THIS BOOK

This book has been written to support students who are new to studying at postgraduate level and who want to understand the difference between studying at Bachelor's level and studying at Master's level. The book may also be useful to those students who would consider themselves established within a postgraduate course but who need to revisit the principles of studying at that level, and may even be a useful resource to those academic staff who are supporting students at Master's level. While we would encourage you to read the book as a complete narrative, you may wish to dip in and out of chapters as your needs arise over the duration of your studies.

Content and coverage

Chapter 1, 'What is Masterly?' This chapter essentially sets the context for the book by introducing the reader to a number of different facts about, and approaches to, postgraduate study. By examining the difference between Bachelor's level and Master's level of study, it seeks to demystify learning outcomes by encouraging the student to consider both the specific personal aims of postgraduate study as well as considering the wider goals of postgraduate education, and to consider how these might be achieved and evidenced.

Chapter 2, 'What is Critical Thinking?' This chapter examines more closely one of the key skills of working and writing at Master's level – that of critical thinking. The concept and theory of critical thinking will be explored and activities will be used to develop students' critical thinking skills.

Chapter 3, 'Becoming an Independent Learner'. This chapter examines the concept of independence as it applies to higher-level study. This is about strategies that the students can employ in order to manage their postgraduate studies effectively and includes support mechanisms for students during their programme of study.

Chapter 4, 'Finding and Critiquing Literature'. This chapter aims to develop students' ability to find high-quality literature, to critique it, to challenge theory, and to apply the findings within debate and argument. The issue of plagiarism will also be considered.

Chapter 5, 'Writing at Master's Level'. This chapter explores the expectations for students' writing at postgraduate level. It covers addressing posed questions, pursuing arguments, structuring the argument, examining the skill of writing interesting and appropriate introductions and conclusions, and considers the use of abstracts. The use of theory, concepts and paradigms is also explored.

Chapter 6, 'How to get Published'. This chapter presents and considers the obligation to share knowledge among the academic community and discusses both tools and tips for getting published.

Chapter 7, 'Applying Postgraduate Knowledge and Skills in the Workplace'. This chapter looks at why it is so important to apply postgraduate skills within the workplace. The concept of employability will be explored and students will be encouraged to examine and develop the skills that make them 'employable'. There is also a discussion of the benefits of Master's thinkers in the workplace, including the impact on improving practice and the quality of care delivery.

THE AUTHORS

Debbie Casey is a senior lecturer in the Faculty of Health and Social Sciences at Leeds Metropolitan University. As a registered nurse she has held a range of senior clinical posts. She has been involved in supporting learning in the practice setting, within an education, development and training department of a large NHS Trust and as a lecturer for the Open University. Her current teaching portfolio includes continuing professional development for health and social care professionals across a range of academic levels. She holds an MA in health care studies.

Liz Clark is a Principal Lecturer in the Faculty of Health and Social Sciences at Leeds Metropolitan University, with wide experience of teaching undergraduate and postgraduate students within nursing and health and social care. Prior to working in higher education she held a range of senior clinical and educational posts within a large NHS Trust. Her current teaching portfolio includes leadership and management, health policy, professional and legal issues and supporting learners in practice. She is a course leader for a Master's level programme and holds an MSc in health professional education.

Sally Hayes is a Head of School in the Faculty of Health and Social Sciences at Leeds Metropolitan University, with experience of teaching students at different academic levels within nursing and health care related professions. Her Master's level education was an MA in management and leadership with the Nuffield Institute of Leeds University and this was undertaken while working as a lead nurse in a Primary Care Trust. Her current portfolio is focused particularly around primary health care provision and includes health policy, leadership, management and enterprise and the development of practice teachers. She is particularly interested in facilitating the development of practitioners who base their practice on a journey of lifelong learning through critical reflection. Her own journey is currently focused on completion of a Taught Doctorate in Education with Sheffield University.

1

WHAT IS MASTERLY?

This chapter covers the following key issues:

- the opportunities that Master's level study offers students;
- consideration of the issues Master's level students face during their studies;
- types of Master's level courses;
- the difference between Bachelor's and Master's level study and outcomes;
- the regulation of higher education and the role of the Quality Assurance Agency for Higher Education (QAA);
- types of content, structure and delivery;
- the types of assessment, learning and teaching students may experience.

By the end of this chapter you should be able to:

- understand the different types of Master's courses available;
- explain the differences between Bachelor's and Master's level courses in terms of what is expected of you as the student;
- describe the role of the QAA;
- explain how Master's courses may be structured and delivered;
- describe the types of assessment, learning and teaching methods that you might encounter.

INTRODUCTION

Relatively little literature exists regarding the transition to postgraduate study, and the research or literature to support learning that is available tends to focus on doctoral study. O'Donnell *et al.* (2009) surmise that this may be based on an assumption that once students graduate with their first degree, postgraduate-level study simply represents 'more of the same', or 'taking things to the next level', and that therefore there is little (if anything) in the way of a transition to be undertaken. As senior lecturers supporting students to take that leap into Master's level study, we disagree with this assumption. Furthermore, we support findings from the research that suggest that difficulties in the transition to postgraduate study are experienced as difficulties in the mastery of key skills or academic practices, suggesting that postgraduate students do not come 'equipped' for their studies in higher education (O'Donnell *et al.*, 2009). Students come to Master's level study with very different expectations and experiences and with different levels of skills in areas such as writing, use of information technology (IT) and even in their ability to access and identify relevant literature. The standard use of virtual learning environments (VLEs) such as, for example, Web CT and X-Stream, can therefore be quite a challenge to some students whose IT skills simply have not kept pace with advancements since completing their Bachelor's degree. However, the most common anecdotal anxiety is 'What is different about Master's level study and what does Master's level writing look like?' This book is therefore intended to support students who are new to Master's level study and who are seeking help in understanding what is expected of them and the challenges that will be coming their way.

STUDYING AT MASTER'S LEVEL

There are many reasons why individuals who already have a Bachelor's degree wish to undertake further study at Master's level. Some of these reasons may be professional – for example, career development through studying a Master's in advanced practice, in order to develop nursing practice to include assessment, diagnosis and treatment in a nurse practitioner role or a consultant therapist role. Other reasons might include: looking for competitive advantage at interview; a love of reading; a wish to recapture the experience of university life and education; or simply a lust for learning. All of these reasons may apply as motivations for professionals from health and social care backgrounds. However, there may be further reasoning. In professions where learning is recognised and valued as driving quality and where reflective practice is a reality, individuals often need the space that academic study can give to stop, unravel, examine and re-create understanding and solutions to the everyday problems that they face in practice. They are looking for the opportunity to face those problems as a 'master'. But what does this mean; what is 'masterly'? Why does undertaking Master's level study make a difference to the ways in which health and social care practitioners think and practise and, importantly, in what ways does it benefit patients and service users?

Various types of Master's degrees exist in the UK, reflecting the independent nature of higher education institutions and the diversity of traditions that exist within different disciplines. For students, this means that there are no nationally agreed definitions of types of award and also that awards with similar titles can vary in nature both between institutions and across disciplines. However, all Master's degrees are expected to meet the generic statement of outcomes set out by the Quality Assurance Agency for Higher

Education (QAA) in the qualification descriptor within *The Framework for Higher Education Qualifications in England, Wales and Northern Ireland* (August 2008) that is examined below, or *The Framework for Qualifications of Higher Education Institutions in Scotland* (January 2001). The qualification descriptor sets out broad expected outcomes for a Master's degree in terms of what graduates should be able to demonstrate and the wider abilities that they would be expected to have developed.

According to the QAA, the opportunities that Master's study offers students include the following:

1. Focusing on a particular aspect of a broader subject area in which they have prior knowledge or experience, whether through previous study or employment.
2. Focusing on a particular subject area or field of study in greater depth than they encountered during the course of previous study or experience.
3. Learning how to conduct research, often linked to a particular discipline or field of study. Such programmes often include a greater emphasis on the delivery of structured learning as opposed to independent study.
4. Undertaking a research project on a topic within the area of interest that makes up the majority of the overall assessment and is normally undertaken with little structured learning.
5. Specialising or becoming more highly specialised in an area of employment or practice related to a particular profession.

(adapted from QAA, 2009)

Furthermore, in the UK three broad and different 'types' of Master's degrees are often described and have been defined by the QAA in their publication *Master's Degree Characteristics* (QAA, 2010). These types are:

1. research Master's;
2. specialised/advanced study Master's;
3. professional/practice Master's.

The QAA classifies them using:

- programme characteristics;
- programme purposes;
- intended entrants;
- relation to further study or employment;
- characteristics of graduates.

The following descriptors are adapted from the QAA's document *Master's Degree Characteristics* (QAA, 2010).

1. Research Master's – for example, the MPhil

- The characteristics of the programmes in this category are that they are typically of one to two years' duration, with two years being most common (based on a full-time mode of study). The research component is larger than the taught component and the student normally conducts a research project through independent study with the inclusion of a smaller 'taught' element like, for example, research methods modules. Assessment is often specific to the individual and likely to be via oral examination that involves discussion/ defence of a thesis, dissertation or other output such as an artefact, performance or musical composition. Research Master's are less common than other types in health and social care.
- The purpose of the programme is to prepare students for the next stage in their careers, whether pursuing further research or entering employment of different kinds, and to enable those undertaking the programme to contribute towards research in the discipline.
- The type of entrant (or admission requirement) is defined by the institution but often requires a Bachelor's degree with honours in a cognate or closely related subject, although experience through work or other means may also be considered appropriate.
- In terms of further study or employment, graduates of Research Master's programmes will normally be prepared to enter a variety of types of employment or to continue to doctoral study.
- Graduates typically have subject-specific attributes including an in-depth knowledge and understanding of the discipline informed by current scholarship and research, the ability to study independently in the subject, and the ability to use a range of techniques and research methods applicable to advanced scholarship in the subject, plus generic attributes such as communication skills.

2. Specialised/advanced study Master's – for example, the MSc, MA, MRes and integrated Master's

- The characteristics of the programmes in this category are that they are often 'taught' although, frequently, at least a third of the programme is devoted to a research project or dissertation. They are typically of 9 to 18 months' duration based on a full-time mode of study. These programmes include integrated Master's degrees (integrated with study at the level of a Bachelor's with honours degree within a single programme) and they also include the MRes, where the student develops the ability to conduct research through a programme of structured learning.
- The purpose of the programme is to prepare students for the next stage in their careers, whether that is further academic or professional study, or entering employment of different kinds.
- The type of entrant (or admission requirement) is again defined by the institution, but entrants often have a background in the subject or a cognate subject area acquired through previous study (a Bachelor's with honours degree or equivalent) or experience.

- In terms of further study or employment, graduates of specialised/ advanced Master's programmes will normally be equipped to enter doctoral study in their discipline or to take up employment in both subject-related and generalist environments.
- Graduates typically have subject-specific attributes and an in-depth knowledge and understanding of the discipline informed by current scholarship and research, including a critical awareness of current issues and developments in the subject as well as a range of generic abilities and skills.

3. Professional/practice Master's – for example, the MBA and MEd

- The characteristics of the programmes in this category are that learning tends to be very structured and this programme structure may be developed in collaboration with the relevant professional, statutory or regulatory body and may include practical elements, such as fieldwork, placements or other opportunities for work-based learning. They are typically of 9 to 24 months' duration based on a full-time mode of study and may be a prerequisite for registration or entry to a profession in accordance with the requirements of the professional, statutory or regulatory body that recognises or accredits the award. In addition, other awards, such as postgraduate certificate and postgraduate diploma, will often be offered alongside professional Master's programmes to facilitate continuing professional development at different stages of a professional career.
- The purpose of the programme is to enable graduates to qualify for entry into a profession, subject to any further conditions required by the professional, statutory or regulatory body and/or provide continuing professional development opportunities related to particular professions or employment settings.
- The type of entrant (or admission requirement) is defined by the institution, taking into account the relevant professional, statutory or regulatory body's requirements, and programmes often attract entrants with a Bachelor's degree with honours (or equivalent) or experience, which may or may not be directly relevant to the particular profession.
- In terms of further study or employment, graduates will normally be equipped to enter a variety of types of employment and, in particular, will possess the skills and experience necessary for the specific profession. They will also normally be equipped to continue academic study at a higher level, for example for a PhD.
- Graduates of professional/practice Master's degrees typically have subject-specific attributes including an in-depth knowledge and understanding of their profession and the ability to apply research to professional situations, both practical and theoretical.

Finally, it must be acknowledged that there are many opportunities for continuing professional development (CPD) at Master's level in addition to full Master's programmes. Individual Master's level modules are also available as part of CPD programmes. However, whatever form the programme takes, it should be distinct from undergraduate study in that it is not 'more of the same' but takes the student 'beyond' undergraduate learning.

ACTIVITY

Access your local university's postgraduate prospectus and find out which Master's courses they offer. How do these relate to the three types of Master's courses described above?

BEING A MASTER'S STUDENT

There are also a number of themes that have been identified about Master's study that it is important to consider. In an ethnographic study of postgraduate students by Tobbell *et al.* (2008), themes that were identified included the following.

Policy

There is a clear difference in approach to undergraduate and postgraduate study within the UK, with a governmental finance framework to support undergraduate students (student loans, fee framework, grants for less-advantaged students, etc.). Universities benefit financially from meeting agreed targets for undergraduate student recruitment while, in contrast, postgraduate students are responsible for identifying their own sources of funding, with a limited number of sources of financial support being available through specific institutions, professional bodies or employers.

Academic status

The postgraduate students in Tobbell *et al.*'s (2008) study reported feeling an enhanced sense of their academic status within the university in contrast to their undergraduate experience, and relationships with staff were more collegiate and more informal.

University systems

Perhaps because the majority of funding is for undergraduates, who represent the majority of the student body, postgraduate students reported that university facilities reflect full-time undergraduate patterns of study. Postgraduate patterns of study differ. Programmes do not necessarily run in normal working hours, with evening and weekend classes being used and, indeed, some postgraduate programmes are taught exclusively in the evening and weekends to accommodate the fact that postgraduate students are often working full-time alongside their studies to finance them.

ACTIVITY

Consider your Master's course or the course you are considering taking. How have you funded/will you fund the course? What hours does the course run over and how does this fit with your personal or work commitments?

What impact did or will the funding and the taught hours have on your decision to enrol?

Life outside the course

Most Master's students face a range of issues that need to be negotiated and problems that need to be addressed in order to enable them to participate fully in their studies. There is no escaping the interaction of normal life and the course, and it could be argued that engagement in university practice can depend on the negotiations that take place in order to deal with the complex demands of students' lives. Data research (Tobbell *et al.*, 2008) shows that, to a greater or lesser extent, Master's students from the first term of study struggle with the demands of 'real' life and study life. This can be dependent on being in employment or, for mature students, having family commitments. Many postgraduate students are giving up time and money, which indicates a commitment and involvement with the process, but this exists in parallel with the tensions of family demands and self-denial (Tobbell *et al.*, 2008).

ACTIVITY

Many universities have significant resources to help students who are experiencing difficulties. Think about your university or place of work. Who would you approach if you were experiencing a personal or financial issue that was impacting on your ability to attend the course?

Pedagogic practice and participation

Participation in postgraduate study requires active desire and considerable motivation. The postgraduate students in Tobbell's research reported greater levels of motivation and active participation in their studies than they had experienced as undergraduates, facilitated by smaller class sizes where there is opportunity for interaction and activity. More emphasis is placed upon autonomous learning, learning through discussion and activity, collaborative learning and independence from ideas and approaches of tutors. The pedagogic practices used on Master's courses, particularly to develop critical thinking skills, will be further discussed in Chapter 2.

WHAT IS 'MASTERLY'?

The whole crux of Master's level work is that the student shows a degree of 'mastery' in an area under investigation. Denby *et al.* (2008) give a clear framework for what this actually means:

- Masters demonstrate that they know what is written about the area (through literature review).
- They can discuss its features and failings and recognise the points of consent and contention (criticality).
- They can examine their own practice (through reflection).
- They can act as a change agent by using their examination to change practice (reflective practitioner).

What is the difference between degree level and Master's level study?

The word 'degree' comes from the Latin word *gradus* meaning 'step' – a step towards achieving mastery in a subject and towards understanding the truth about their particular academic discipline. Masters are not, therefore, expected to merely assimilate knowledge, but to explore the parameters of their particular subject area in order to achieve 'mastery'. For health and social care professionals, this must also mean that they can bring their 'mastery' to bear on their own professional practice.

ACTIVITY

Think about the abilities that you would expect someone in your profession to exhibit if they had truly become a master of their professional area. It may help you to think in terms of:

- their knowledge;
- their skills;
- their behaviours and/or attitudes.

How are these different from the knowledge, skills and behaviours of someone who had studied only as far as degree level?

Regulation of higher education

As referred to previously, it is important to remember that the curriculum of higher education (HE) courses is closely regulated. The primary responsibility for academic standards and quality in UK HE rests with individual universities and colleges, each of which is independent and self-governing. However, the Quality Assurance Agency for Higher Education (QAA) checks how well they meet their responsibilities, identifying good practice and making recommendations for improvement. The QAA publishes a set of reference points, known as the UK Quality Code for Higher Education, which institutions use in maintaining academic standards and quality. The Quality Code comprises three components: Part A: Setting and maintaining threshold academic standards; Part B: Assuring and enhancing academic quality; and Part C: Information about higher education provision (QAA, 2012; available at **www.qaa.ac.uk/AssuringStandardsAndQuality/ quality-code/Pages/default.aspx**). These published guidelines help institutions develop effective systems to ensure students have high-quality experiences. Part of this guidance is a clear framework for the standards required at different academic levels.

The QAA describes Master's degrees as 'academic qualifications located at level 7 (M level)' in *The FHEQ in England, Wales and Northern Ireland* (August 2008), and at level 11 in *The Framework for Qualifications of Higher Education Institutions in Scotland* (January 2001). All Master's degrees are expected to meet the national qualification descriptor, which is a statement of the nature and level of the outcomes of study (QAA, 2009). Subject benchmark statements set out expectations about standards of degrees in a range of subject areas. They express what can be expected of graduates in terms of the abilities and skills needed to develop understanding or competence in the subject. The QAA publishes a small number of subject benchmark statements for Master's degrees that readers can consult on their website (**www.qaa.ac.uk**) but these currently relate to only a minority of subject areas (see Figure 1).

In addition, a detailed description of an individual programme of study specific to a particular higher education institution should be available in the form of a programme

---

Business and Management

Chemistry

Dentistry

Engineering

Mathematics, statistics and operational research

Medicine

Pharmacy

Physics

Veterinary science

www.qaa.ac.uk/AssuringStandardsAndQuality/subject-guidance/Pages/Master%27s-degree-benchmark- statements.aspx

---

Figure 1. *QAA Master's level benchmark statements*

specification produced by that institution. Students on all courses must pay careful attention to this in order to be absolutely sure of the details of the programme and that these details fit with the outcomes they require.

Examining *The Framework for Higher Education Qualifications in England, Wales and Northern Ireland* (August 2008)

This is what the QAA says about Degree (honours) level degrees and graduates:

> Honours degrees form the largest group of higher education qualifications. Typical courses last for three years (if taken full-time) and lead to a Bachelors degree with Honours, having a title such as Bachelor of Arts (BA (Hons)) or Bachelor of Science (BSc (Hons)). Also at this level are short courses and professional 'conversion' courses, based largely on undergraduate material, and taken usually by those who are already graduates in another discipline, leading to Graduate Certificates or Graduate Diplomas.
>
> An Honours graduate will have developed an understanding of a complex body of knowledge, some of it at the current boundaries of an academic discipline. Through this, the graduate will have developed analytical techniques and problem-solving skills that can be applied in many types of employment. The graduate will be able to evaluate evidence, arguments and assumptions, to reach sound judgements, and to communicate effectively.
>
> An Honours graduate should have the qualities needed for employment in situations requiring the exercise of personal responsibility, and decision-making in complex and unpredictable circumstances.

> (QAA, 2008)

ACTIVITY

Think back to your degree course.

- What was the body of knowledge you studied?
- How did you develop analytical techniques and problem-solving skills?
- How did it prepare you for personal responsibility and decision-making?

This is what the QAA says about Master's level study:

> Much of the study undertaken at Master's level will have been at, or informed by, the forefront of an academic or professional discipline. Students will have shown originality in the application of knowledge, and they will understand how the boundaries of knowledge are advanced through research. They will be able to deal

with complex issues both systematically and creatively, and they will show originality in tackling and solving problems.

They will have the qualities needed for employment in circumstances requiring sound judgement, personal responsibility and initiative, in complex and unpredictable professional environments.

(QAA, 2008)

ACTIVITY

Can you identify the difference between the achievements described by the QAA at degree level and those at Master's? Think of one or two key words that capture the difference.

The QAA goes on to give more detailed descriptors for the award of honours degrees and Master's. Table 1 enables you to compare the descriptors. We have underlined some of the key differences at Master's degree level to make your comparison easier.

Table 1

Honours degrees are awarded to students who have demonstrated:	Master's degrees are awarded to students who have demonstrated:
1. A systematic understanding of key aspects of their field of study, including acquisition of coherent and detailed knowledge, at least some of which is at, or informed by, the forefront of defined aspects of a discipline.	**1.** A systematic understanding of knowledge, and a critical awareness of current problems and/or new insights, much of which is at, or informed by, the forefront of their <u>academic discipline, field of study, or area of professional practice.</u>
2. An ability to deploy accurately established techniques of analysis and enquiry within a discipline.	**2.** A <u>comprehensive understanding</u> of techniques applicable <u>to their own research or advanced scholarship.</u>
3. Conceptual understanding that enables the student: • to devise and sustain arguments, and/or to solve problems, using ideas and techniques, some of which are at the forefront of a discipline; and • to describe and comment upon particular aspects of current research, or equivalent advanced scholarship, in the discipline.	**3.** <u>Originality in the application of knowledge,</u> together with a practical understanding of how established techniques of research and enquiry are used to <u>create and interpret knowledge in the discipline.</u>

4. An appreciation of the uncertainty, ambiguity and limits of knowledge.

5. The ability to manage their own learning, and to make use of scholarly reviews and primary sources (e.g. refereed research articles and/or original materials appropriate to the discipline).

4. Conceptual understanding that enables the student:

- to <u>evaluate critically</u> current research and advanced scholarship in the discipline; and
- to evaluate methodologies and <u>develop critiques</u> of them and, where appropriate, to <u>propose new hypotheses.</u>

Typically, holders of the qualification will be able to:	**Typically, holders of the qualification will be able to:**
A. Apply the methods and techniques that they have learned to review, consolidate, extend and apply their knowledge and understanding, and to initiate and carry out projects.	**A.** Deal with <u>complex issues both systematically and creatively,</u> make <u>sound judgements</u> in the absence of complete data, and communicate their conclusions clearly to specialist and non-specialist audiences.
B. Critically evaluate arguments, assumptions, abstract concepts and data (that may be incomplete), to make judgements, and to frame appropriate questions to achieve a solution – or identify a range of solutions – to a problem.	**B.** <u>Demonstrate self-direction and originality</u> in tackling and solving problems, and act <u>autonomously</u> in planning and implementing tasks at a professional or equivalent level.
C. Communicate information, ideas, problems, and solutions to both specialist and non-specialist audiences.	**C.** <u>Continue to advance</u> their knowledge and understanding, and to develop new skills to a high level.
and will have: **D.** The qualities and transferable skills necessary for employment requiring: • the exercise of initiative and personal responsibility; • decision-making in complex and unpredictable contexts; and • the learning ability needed to undertake appropriate further training of a professional or equivalent nature.	**and will have:** **D.** The qualities and transferable skills necessary for employment requiring: • the exercise of initiative and personal responsibility; • decision-making in complex and unpredictable situations; and • the <u>independent learning</u> ability required for continuing professional development.

(Table adapted from QAA 2008)

ACTIVITY

Reflect on the words/phrase/sections that are underlined in Table 1 and that represent key differences between degree and Master's level awards. What are the recurring themes?

On studying the QAA's detailed descriptors for the award of honours degrees and Master's, the main themes or differences that can be identified relate to:

- the ability of the award holder to practise at the forefront of their academic discipline, field of study, or area of professional practice;
- undertaking their own research or advanced scholarship;
- demonstrating originality in the application of knowledge;
- having a role in creating and interpreting knowledge in their discipline;
- dealing with complex issues both systematically and creatively;
- making sound judgements that demonstrate self-direction and originality;
- acting autonomously and continuing to develop skills through independence;
- evaluating critically and even proposing new hypotheses.

This is how the QAA summarises the capability of Master's graduates:

> In broad terms, graduates of all Master's degrees should be capable of demonstrating a systematic understanding of knowledge, much of which is at, or informed by, the forefront of the discipline, field of study or area of professional practice. They should be capable of demonstrating originality in their application of that knowledge and in addressing problems. They will have demonstrated a comprehensive understanding of the techniques applicable to their own research or advanced scholarship. In relation to future employment, Master's graduates will be expected to possess the skills needed to exercise independent learning and to develop new skills to a high level.

(QAA, 2009, p. 7)

The content, structure and delivery of Master's awards

As stated previously, the content of a Master's degree in terms of the areas of knowledge and understanding, expertise and skills that the student will acquire are defined by the higher education institution (HEI). The content of a programme will be appropriate to the intended purpose of the award. This means that the content or curriculum will reflect the needs of the discipline/field of study, the profession or both. In some cases, especially where the Master's is within a professional field, the content of the degree will be agreed with an employer or professional regulatory body such as the Nursing and

Midwifery Council (NMC) or the Health and Care Professions Council (HCPC), and the professional body will then monitor and regulate delivery through approval of courses and audit.

As previously discussed, Master's degrees are delivered via full- or part-time programmes with varying amounts of face-to-face contact or distance learning. This may be full-time (usually one year) or the equivalent over a part-time trajectory. However, this does vary – the MPhil, for example, often takes up to two years to complete full-time.

It may also be that students are able to use the Credit Accumulation and Transfer Scheme (CATS), which is used by many universities in the United Kingdom to monitor, record and reward passage through modular courses and to facilitate movement between courses and institutions. This approach recognises that Master's degrees may be modular and may incorporate progression through to postgraduate certificate (60 credit points) and diploma (120 credit points). A postgraduate Master's degree is equivalent to 180 points and so, if an individual has been awarded 15 or 20 credits for successful completion of a Master's level module at a different institution, or even awarded a postgraduate certificate or diploma, it may be that these credits can be transferred and effectively used to buy in credit against a whole Master's programme. Universities will have established policies concerning the use of CATS points, and these should be made clear in the admissions policies for different courses or programmes and are usually considered on a case-by-case basis. One element that will normally be considered is 'currency' and this is a judgement about whether the knowledge and learning achieved on the module or course where a student wants to use the CATS is considered by the university as remaining current and valid. A broad definition of this excludes study that is more than five years old.

There will also be an integrated strategy of teaching, learning and assessment that enables the student to demonstrate the intended learning outcomes appropriate to the programme's overall aims.

Learning outcomes

Learning outcomes describe what a student should be able to do in order to successfully complete either a course of study, a module or even a short and specific study session. They describe student activities and attainments (Baume, 2009) and essentially what they should be able to do by the end of the period of study.

They are therefore essential to students on two main levels. The first is in deciding which programme of study to undertake. Do the outcomes of the programme meet or fit with the learning opportunity that you are looking for? Secondly, once enrolled on the course, the individual learning outcomes for the module give a clear summary of what the student needs to demonstrate in order to pass the module. In essence they set out what any module assessment should demonstrate. This is important information that helps students understand exactly what it is that they have to do and learn in order to pass. They should therefore use the learning outcomes to shape and focus their reading and assessed work (Burns and Sinfield, 2004).

Assessment, learning and teaching

The assessment, learning and teaching (ALT) methods to be used will be identified in individual programme documentation, such as a programme specification, and may include a diverse array of methods. Those used will be selected by the institution or academic lead as being most appropriate to the discipline or field of study and the programme's aims, mode of delivery and typical entrants (see Figure 2).

- lectures;
- tutorials;
- seminars;
- practical work, or practice placements;
- the use of textbooks, journal papers, electronic databases;
- individual project work;
- group work;
- practice sessions and learning through case studies;
- work-based learning;
- engagements with virtual learning environments.

Figure 2. *Examples of the ALT methods used on Master's courses*

Assessment

The definition of assessment 'as a generic term for a set of processes that measures the outcomes of students' learning in terms of knowledge acquired, understanding developed, and skills gained' (Quality Assurance Agency for Higher Education, 2000) is arguably too simplistic, as higher levels of learning concern the process that the learner undertakes as well as the outcome of the learning (Hayes and MacKreth, 2008). On professional Master's courses there are several reasons to assess competence, including: to judge 'fitness to practise'; to direct and motivate learning; to ensure the correct standards are achieved before a student progresses to the next level; to provide feedback for students; and to provide feedback on the curriculum and method of delivery (Manogue *et al.*, 2002). Careful planning and management are therefore required to ensure that the goal of using assessment is not only to judge outcome but also to focus on motivating the process of learning.

Another consideration is that, for the duration of a course, account is taken of the difference in individual student preference for assessment methods and learning styles. For example, some students may be very good strategic learners who prefer to sit exams and are very successful at passing them, whereas other students may find exams so stressful that they do very poorly at them due to anxiety. It is therefore important that Master's course designers use different assessment methods during the course in order to acknowledge the different aptitudes of student groups or, alternatively, to ensure that prospective students are able to consider assessment methodologies before enrolling on courses.

There are numerous assessment methods that are used at Master's level (see Figure 3).

- essay assignments and other types of coursework;
- practical reports or portfolios;
- dissertations;
- work-based studies;
- written examinations;
- problem-solving exercises;
- oral presentations;
- posters;
- placement reports.

Figure 3. *Examples of the assessment methods used on Master's courses*

ACTIVITY

Consider the types of assessment on your Master's course.

- How do they measure whether you are achieving the required outcomes of the course?
- How do they motivate you?

SUMMARY

This chapter has introduced Master's level study by examining the types of Master's level courses available and the opportunities that Master's level study offers students in terms of their professional and personal development. More specific examples of these opportunities will be explored and developed in later chapters. Consideration has been made of the issues that Master's level students face during their studies and students are encouraged to examine the resources available at their university to help them face problems and challenges.

An in-depth examination of the difference between Bachelor's and Master's level study and outcomes was made, with the notions of independence, criticality and working at the forefront of practice being identified as key themes.

The regulation of higher education and the role of the Quality Assurance Agency for Higher Education (QAA) were examined and the types of content, structure and delivery, alongside the types of assessment, learning and teaching which students may experience at this higher level of working, were considered.

Critical reflection	
Identify at least three things that you have learned from this chapter.	1. 2. 3.
How do you plan to use this knowledge?	1. 2. 3.
How will you evaluate the effectiveness of your plan?	1. 2. 3.
What further knowledge and evidence do you need?	1. 2. 3.

FURTHER READING

www.qaa.ac.uk
The QAA website contains a plethora of information about how academic institutions are regulated and a whole series of benchmarks for different Master's level qualifications.

2

WHAT IS CRITICAL THINKING?

This chapter covers the following key issues:

- definitions and characteristics of critical thinking;
- the relationship of the development of critical thinking to conceptions of knowledge;
- the importance of critical thinking for health and social care professionals;
- activities to help develop critical thinking skills.

By the end of this chapter you should be able to:

- provide a definition of what critical thinking is;
- discuss how critical thinking is developed through both academic and work-based learning;
- reflect on the importance of critical thinking as a learning outcome for postgraduate students and, in particular, for health and social care students.

INTRODUCTION

Chapter 1 has introduced you to the concept of Master's level study, explored some of the key attributes of postgraduate study and encouraged you to consider some of the issues that postgraduate students face during their studies, particularly relating to delivery and assessment, and to your own personal development goals. This chapter will consider one of the key aims of postgraduate study – the ability to demonstrate critical thinking.

It is worth revisiting some of the broad learning outcomes of postgraduate study specified by the Quality Assurance Agency for Higher Education (QAA) from Chapter 1 (see Figure 1).

Master's degrees are awarded to students who have demonstrated:

- a systematic understanding of knowledge, and a critical awareness of current problems and/or new insights, much of which is at, or informed by, the forefront of their academic discipline, field of study or area of professional practice;
- a comprehensive understanding of techniques applicable to their own research or advanced scholarship;
- originality in the application of knowledge, together with a practical understanding of how established techniques of research and enquiry are used to create and interpret knowledge in the discipline;
- conceptual understanding that enables the student
  - to evaluate critically current research and advanced scholarship in the discipline;
  - to evaluate methodologies and develop critiques.

Figure 1. *Descriptor for a higher education qualification at level 7 Master's degree (source: QAA, 2008)*

The descriptor in Figure 1 shows that Master's level students need to demonstrate more than just comprehensive knowledge of the subject, although that is obviously a key element of gaining mastery of a subject. The terms 'critical awareness', 'evaluate critically' and 'develop critiques' in the QAA learning outcomes suggest the notion of 'being critical'. It is important to review what is meant by this term.

Being critical

Being critical in everyday life may be associated with expressing adverse or disapproving comments on something. Often these criticisms may be fairly subjective and not based on strong evidence or have a clear rationale. In contrast, academic criticism needs to be objective, factual and considered. Your previous experiences as a student will have demonstrated the importance of being fair in your judgements and supporting arguments with available evidence in academic work. Being critical in academic work is not, therefore, the same as criticising in everyday life.

ACTIVITY

Write down what you think 'being critical' means in relation to academic work.

Some suggestions that you have written down might include phrases like:

- not accepting things at face value;
- evaluating;
- making judgements;
- exploring the implications of something;
- making a comparison to other work.

Implicit in all of these phrases is an attempt to recognise the value or quality of something. This may be an idea, a concept, a product or a piece of writing, for example. Being critical in academic terms includes considering both negative and positive aspects. The notion of being critical is not, therefore, something to be undertaken in a superficial or *ad hoc* manner. A critical approach can only be achieved in a considered and systematic way, as it requires reviewing something in some depth and in the context of other work related to the topic or concept under scrutiny.

The ability to 'be critical' implies something that can apply to a one-off act or event – a skill that is demonstrated on a single occasion. However, developing mastery in a subject suggests the development and integration of skills and knowledge leading to new perspectives on how knowledge is viewed. In other words, it leads to a change in how we think – hence 'critical thinking'. To start to 'be critical' is therefore just the start of becoming a critical thinker, which suggests an approach or disposition to think critically in all aspects of life. Daly (2001) has stated that 'Most commentators agree that a repertoire of knowledge and discrete skills is of little use if it lies redundant or is used selectively' (Daly, 2001, p. 121).

In other words, critical thinkers exhibit the habit of thinking critically as part of their intellectual repertoire. They are likely to demonstrate a spirit of enquiry and a questioning attitude in order to probe deeper into something to develop their own knowledge base and understanding.

WHAT IS CRITICAL THINKING?

There is a considerable body of literature on the concept of critical thinking and there is a wide range of definitions. There does not, however, appear to be one universally accepted definition of what the concept is, although within the literature some defining characteristics emerge.

The concept of critical thinking is widely acknowledged to have its origins in the historical work of John Dewey, an educationalist and psychologist who wrote his seminal work *How We Think* in 1910. Dewey described critical thinking as reflective thinking that is:

> Active, persistent, and careful consideration of any belief or supposed form of knowledge in the light of the grounds that support it and the further conclusion to which it tends.

> (Dewey, 1910, cited in McGregor, 2007)

We will return to the concept of reflection and its relationship to critical thinking at the end of this chapter, but it is worth analysing some of the key words in Dewey's definition.

Active

The critical thinker is fully engaged in the process – the individual must personally consider the issues, question the underlying assumptions and scrutinise the evidence, as opposed to learning in a passive way by being told by someone else. Indeed, much of the literature on critical thinking is about challenging educators to adopt and develop innovative teaching methodologies to promote critical thinking skills in students.

ACTIVITY

Consider the ways in which the lecturers on your postgraduate course facilitate your learning to support your active engagement in the learning process – consider the teaching style, the educational approaches, methodologies and activities, and the assessment processes.

Persistent

This echoes Daly's point, referred to earlier, that the skills of critical thinking are not used intermittently or selectively (Daly, 2001) but that they are integrated into all aspects of learning and become a way of engaging with the world.

There seems to be another implication in the use of the word 'persistent' that suggests the critical thinker does not give up the quest to find the right answer easily, but doggedly pursues a subject until satisfied that all possible questions have been answered.

Grounds that support it

This refers to the evidence base that must be subject to a healthy scepticism and carefully evaluated. This may include the need to utilise critical appraisal skills. Critical appraisal has been described as the process of carefully and systematically examining research to judge its trustworthiness, and its value and relevance in a particular context (Burls, 2009). A range of tools are available to support the process – the use of these will be discussed in Chapter 4 on 'Finding and critiquing literature'.

The further conclusion

Critical thinking is therefore outcome-orientated in that, through reasoned thinking, a conclusion is pursued. However, it is important to be aware that the conclusion may not in itself provide an unequivocal answer to a question or a resolution to an issue. The conclusion may be an increased understanding of the issue and acceptance of ambiguity (Daly, 1998).

This latter point is well illustrated if we consider the example of a researcher undertaking a systematic review of the evidence of the effectiveness of a particular intervention or treatment. This process will include:

- identifying all relevant published and unpublished evidence;
- selecting the studies or reports by assessing their individual quality against specific inclusion criteria;
- synthesising the findings from individual studies or reports in an unbiased way;
- interpreting the findings and presenting a balanced and impartial summary of the findings with due consideration of any flaws in the evidence.

However, even though the critical process of reaching an objective conclusion has clearly been undertaken in a systematic way, it may be that there is inadequate evidence to extrapolate a definitive conclusion on the effectiveness of the intervention or treatment. That is not to say that the intervention is ineffective – but that there is an absence of evidence demonstrating its effectiveness. Hence the need to tolerate ambiguity while, of course, being aware that the implications are that there is a need for further robust research to provide a definitive answer.

This leads us to consider the differences between pure problem-solving and critical thinking. Critical thinking may be part of the process of problem-solving but may not lead to a solution. To the critical thinker, assumptions about the outcome do not exist; therefore problem-solving follows a different process. Facione *et al.* (1994) summarise this by suggesting that critical thinking is ultimately a cognitive engine that drives problem-solving and decision-making.

Therefore, if we accept Dewey's definition, critical thinking is essentially about evaluating the worth, accuracy or authenticity of something through a critical review of the evidence. This is likely to lead to a supportable decision or direction for action.

More recent definitions of what critical thinking is echo Dewey's definition and include:

> Critical thinking is not one single way of thinking, but rather it is multi-dimensional cognitive process. It demands a skilful application of knowledge and experience in making discriminating judgements and evaluations.

> (Jones and Brown, 1991, p. 530)

And:

> the rational examination of ideas, inferences, principles, arguments, conclusions, issues, structures, beliefs and actions.

> (Bandman and Bandman, 1995, p. 7)

Bandman and Bandman (1995) add a qualifying statement to their definition in which they say that critical thinkers are also self-aware and sympathetic to others. They need to be open-minded in that there needs to be a willingness to respect the rights of others to hold different opinions. This is interesting because it adds a human dimension to the definition. This makes sense if we consider that to think critically means the individual must be aware of the problems of bias or incomplete reasoning. If we are to be logical, we must therefore recognise our own biases and engage in some critique of our own reasoning processes. In this way there is an element of being self-regulatory by monitoring one's own thinking.

ACTIVITY

Have a look at some of the wider literature on critical thinking and review some of the definitions. Are there any emerging themes or commonalities?

The diverse and differing number of definitions may seem daunting initially. However, it is worth considering what the different definitions have in common. Daly (2001) has suggested that there are four fundamental constituents of critical thinking and these provide a useful starting point for understanding what it means. They are:

- a pre-requisite knowledge base;
- a series of intellectual skills;
- a disposition to use both knowledge and skills in scrutinising and evaluating information;
- a series of intellectual standards to which such thinking should conform.

(Daly, 2001, p. 121)

ACTIVITY

Refer back to the broad learning outcomes of postgraduate study specified by the Quality Assurance Agency for Higher Education (QAA) reported at the beginning of this chapter. How do they match up with Daly's 'fundamental constituents' of critical thinking?

The first constituent of critical thinking suggested by Daly, a pre-requisite knowledge base, needs little comment as it is clearly essential to have a fundamental understanding of a subject in order that meaningful connections can be made between new and existing knowledge cumulatively. The third constituent, the disposition to use knowledge and skills, bringing a critical dimension to all aspects of life – in other words, becoming aware of fallacious arguments, ambiguity, and manipulative reasoning – has already been discussed.

However, both the second and final constituents – what intellectual skills are required of the critical thinker and the intellectual standards that critical thinkers must adhere to – require some further exploration.

Intellectual skills exhibited by the critical thinker

ACTIVITY

List five intellectual skills that you think the critical thinker should exhibit.

Facione *et al.* (1994) postulated that if a specific attitude or disposition towards critical thinking is not evident, then the critical thinking skills will not be used. To this end, Facione developed a tool for measuring an individual's disposition to critical thinking. This is known as the Californian Critical Thinking Disposition Inventory and has been used quite widely in research to assess critical thinking disposition (Shin *et al.*, 2006). The inventory focuses on the key attributes:

- open-mindedness;
- inquisitiveness;
- truth-seeking;
- analyticity;
- systematicity;
- self-confidence;
- maturity of judgement.

These are interesting personal characteristics that you might want to consider in terms of self-evaluation and your own disposition towards using critical thinking skills. However, for a more specific skills-based list of the skills themselves, it might be useful to look to educational theory and, in particular, to the work of Bloom.

Bloom was an educational psychologist who devised a classification or taxonomy that attempted to articulate different intellectual behaviours and different levels of expertise in learning (Stuart, 2007). He identified three learning domains:

- Cognitive: knowledge acquisition;
- Affective: emotions and feeling;
- Psycho-motor: skill demonstration.

It is Bloom's taxonomy for the cognitive domain that has particular relevance to the characteristics of critical thinking. Bloom postulated that in the cognitive domain, 'thinking' abilities could be measured along a continuum running from simple to complex. Knowledge was considered to be a fundamental cognitive skill, whereas synthesis and evaluation were skills that Bloom felt demonstrated higher-order thinking skills (see Figure 2).

- Knowledge
- Comprehension
- Application
- Analysis
- Synthesis
- Evaluation

Figure 2. *Bloom's taxonomy (Bloom, 1956, cited in Stuart, 2007)*

You may recognise these characteristics as competencies or outcomes that you are required to demonstrate in your module or programme descriptors.

ACTIVITY

Write a definition for each of the terms in Bloom's taxonomy.

While it might be reasonable to question the hierarchical nature of the taxonomy, it does still provide a very useful list of skills that students are expected to demonstrate under the umbrella term of 'critical thinking'.

Bloom's taxonomy is particularly useful when educationalists are considering the assessment of the different academic competencies. Stuart (2007) has drawn up a list of 'question words' for use in assessment and argues that they should reveal to the learner both the kind of thinking expected, and the stimulation of different types of thinking.

ACTIVITY

Compare and contrast your own definitions with the explanations of the terms provided in Figure 3. Consider how useful the 'question words' suggested by Stuart are in signposting the student to the type of academic skills required in an answer.

Knowledge: those processes which require recall of such things as specific facts, terminology, conventions and generalisations.
Words: what, when, which, identify, describe, define, list.

Comprehension: a level of understanding sufficient to grasp the translation and meaning of material for the purpose of interpretation or extrapolation.
Words: compare, contrast, differentiate, explain, extrapolate.

Application: employs remembering, problem-solving and combining material to give generalisation for use in concrete situations.
Words: apply, consider, how would, utilise.

Analysis: the breakdown of material into its constituents in order to explore the relationships between them.
Words: support your, what assumptions, what reasons.

Synthesis: demonstrating creativity by the putting together of the constituents, rearranging or combining them to give an arrangement not apparent before.
Words: think of a way, create, plan, suggest.

Evaluation: requires value judgements about material, ideas and methods.
Words: judge, consider, defend, which would.

Figure 3. *Question words (Stuart, 2007)*

We will return to these terms in Chapter 5 when we explore ways of demonstrating critical thinking in written work.

The intellectual standards to which critical thinking should conform

The final constituent suggested by Daly is the series of intellectual standards that a critical thinker applies. Paul and Elder (2008) have provided a definition of critical thinking that emphasises this characteristic:

> Critical thinking is that mode of thinking – about any subject, content, or problem – in which the thinker improves the quality of his or her thinking by skilfully taking charge of the structures inherent in thinking and imposing intellectual standards upon them.

> (Paul and Elder, 2008, p. 4)

ACTIVITY

Consider Paul and Elder's (2008) definition of critical thinking. What type of 'intellectual standards' do you think Paul and Elder might be suggesting should be used to improve the quality of your thinking?

Paul and Elder have suggested that 'good thinking' about a problem, issue or situation is distinguished from non-critical thinking by a number of characteristics.

- **Clarity** – this is a gateway standard. In other words, if thinking is not clear or not able to be clearly articulated, then others will not be able to access your ideas or thoughts, so it is an absolute criterion.

- **Accuracy** – facts must be checked and statements supported by robust evidence.

- **Precision** – specific details are given to enable the nature or scope of the issue to be recognised.

- **Relevance** – only issues with a clear relationship or connection to the issue are considered.

- **Depth** – the complexities of the issue are dealt with or explored.

- **Breadth** – wider issues or other perspectives are considered.

- **Logic** – thoughts are coherent and mutually supportive and add up to provide an intelligently constructed narrative.

Compare these standards to your own ideas on intellectual standards. We will return to these in Chapter 5 (Writing at Master's Level) when we look at demonstrating some of these criteria in academic writing.

CONCEPTIONS OF KNOWLEDGE

Moon (2008), in her useful book that provides an exploration of the theory and practice of critical thinking, has linked the development of critical thinking skills to the learner's developing conception of what knowledge is – sometimes called epistemological development. Moon cites the work of Baxter Magolda (1992), who studied college students and identified a continuum of how knowledge is viewed by students, utilising four domains to describe the different perspectives on knowledge.

- **Absolute knowing** – the student views knowledge as absolute or certain, and formal learning is a matter of absorption of the knowledge of experts.

- **Transitional knowing** – the student begins to have doubts about the certainty of knowledge and acknowledges that there is both partial certainty and partial uncertainty.

- **Independent knowing** – the student recognises the uncertainty of knowledge, and copes with this by taking the position that everyone has a right to his or her own opinion or belief.

- **Contextual knowing** – the student understands that knowledge is contracted and understood in relation to the effective deployment of evidence that best fits a given context.

(Baxter Magolda, 1992, described in Moon, 2008, p. 103)

Consider how a student at the stage of 'absolute knowing' might view the role of the teacher in supporting his or her learning. Contrast this to the way the student who has reached the stage of 'contextual knowing' might understand the role of teacher to be.

It is likely that the student who views knowledge as certain or absolute would expect the teacher to be the expert who imparts knowledge in quite a didactic way, with little scope for discussion as facts are seen as right or wrong. However, the more developed student, who accepts that all knowledge is contextual, would see the teacher as facilitator and partner in learning.

Baxter Magolda's four domains of 'knowing' seem to be a particularly useful way of considering the development of thinking in a postgraduate student. Clearly students need to be at the stage of 'contextual knowing' to achieve Master's level outcomes and, in particular, to think critically. A student who does not recognise the importance of context in relation to knowledge will not exhibit some of the characteristics of critical thinking suggested in the previous section. This can also be illustrated in the following activity.

Imagine two students are undertaking a university module and are asked to undertake an assignment exploring truth-telling and a professional's obligations to patients/clients.

- Student A is at the stage of 'absolute knowing'.
- Student B is at the stage of 'contextual knowing'.

Consider how the different conceptual stages in their understanding may be manifest in their written work.

Student A is likely to accept the obligation to tell the truth as an absolute rule that is not challenged but accepted unquestioningly. This means that Student A's written work may be at the very descriptive stage, providing a unilateral view of the topic, accepting the concept without dispute, and may not explore the wider implications of any findings. Student A may also struggle to develop their own opinions or standpoint on the issue of truth-telling. In contrast, Student B will probably acknowledge that although the obligation to tell the truth to patients/service users is important, that obligation may be moderated or dependent on context – such as a situation where an individual's mental health or emotional wellbeing may be damaged by giving them certain information at that specific time. Student B recognises that there are times when absolute rules depend on context. Student B's work is therefore likely to be discursive and exploratory; it will provide alternative perspectives on the topic. It may challenge and critique concepts, ideas and findings and it considers the wider implications of any findings. The student can then develop personal ideas and views from the work undertaken.

The student at this stage of 'contextual knowing' understands that, while all knowledge has an objective element, it is also mediated by, or dependent on, a number of factors. In other words, it is shaped by such issues as the historical context, in relation to other knowledge and the nature of the experience or issue to which it is being applied. Knowles (1980), building on his seminal work on the adult learner, stated that 'facts learned in your youth have become insufficient and in many instances are actually untrue' (Knowles, 1980, p. 28). 'Contextual' in this sense therefore, refers to acknowledging that the usefulness of information will depend on when and where and how it is applied. This is particularly important for practitioners working in health and social care where exposure to new information – in the form of policy imperatives, guidelines, research and literature – is occurring on a regular basis.

ACTIVITY

Imagine the following scenario.

You have come across an interesting piece of research in which the findings suggest that a particular intervention that you undertake in your practice may be unhelpful in achieving optimum outcomes for your patients/service users/clients. Assuming the quality of the research is sound, what are some of the contextual issues that you are likely to think about in deciding whether to take any actions on the findings?

Here are some of the issues you might have included in your list.

- Time of publication – does the research fully reflect current practice or have changes been made that mean the findings are no longer applicable?
- Other relevant research – what does other research show – does it support or contrast the findings?
- National guidelines on the practice – does the research contradict national guidance – what are the implications if it does?
- Local context – is there anything in the local practice that means the findings are not relevant? For example, specific issues relating to the client/patient group, specific characteristics of the staff group involved, etc.
- Are there pragmatic reasons why it is not practical to apply the findings? These might include funding issues.

In other words, a range of contextual issues that give you a different perspective on that information need to be considered.

Obviously this is, to some extent, an oversimplification of a complex subject – and Moon herself reports that Baxter Magolda observed that students could shift between the four domains – moving forwards and occasionally backwards as they encounter different challenges to their learning (Moon, 2008, p. 103). However, what is important is succinctly summarised by Moon: 'Fully developed critical thinking involves making a judgement, and involves an inherent recognition that knowledge is contestable' (Moon, 2008, p. 112).

THE LINK TO CREATIVE THINKING

When we consider critical thinking it is important to consider the role of creativity.

ACTIVITY

What terms or words do you associate with creativity in relation to academic thinking?

Some of the terms you might have generated in your list include: being original, innovating, thinking 'outside the box', mind-mapping, making new and unusual connections and associations, thinking widely, applying concepts or ideas in a novel way, or identifying different relationships. Certainly the skill of synthesis described earlier is strongly associated with being creative.

Academics sometimes discuss written work submitted by students as competent but dull – in other words it lacks any sort of originality or different 'take' on a subject. Thus creativity is more than just the generation of new ideas – it is the ability to bring something new to the 'academic' table.

Creativity is clearly different to critical thinking and Daly (1998) makes the point that although there is a relationship between the two concepts, there is also a clear difference between the two: 'Creativity by its generative nature can proceed initially from a blank sheet, critical thinking cannot. The two forms of thinking do, however, converge' (Daly, 1998, p. 324).

What Daly appears to be suggesting is that, while creativity has the potential to be demonstrated spontaneously at any time, the process of critical thinking is undertaken systematically and, as it is about evaluating, it requires information or data or an idea as a starting point. Where the two concepts overlap is in the process of the critical thinker reaching a considered and balanced standpoint on an issue or problem. This is likely to require the generation of alternative views or the development of new ideas, concepts or theories, thus utilising creative or imaginative skills. In this way the two notions of critical thinking and creativity converge.

This can be illustrated if we consider the role of a researcher in testing out a hypothesis. The researcher clearly utilises the skills of the critical thinker in systematically testing out a hypothesis or research question, but they must also use the skills of creativity in both the development and choice of appropriate research methodologies and in interpreting and making inferences from the data. Both critical thinking and creativity centre on the importance of independent thought.

WHY IS CRITICAL THINKING IMPORTANT?

Critical thinking is clearly important beyond the world of academia. It is a skill used in a variety of situations in that it enables us to make informed decisions about events and issues in our everyday life – such as making choices about our lifestyle or attempting to understand the behaviour of others. Critical thinking therefore appears to be a desirable characteristic for all human beings in that it is associated with tolerance and rational decision-making. Taylor (2000) suggests that it 'turns an unconsidered life to one that is consciously aware, self-potentiating and purposeful' (Taylor, 2000, p. 10).

These are clearly crucial skills for the health or social care professional faced with an increasingly complex world where there are not always single or absolutely correct responses. The skills of critical thinking in practice in the work environment will be explored in detail in Chapter 6 on 'Applying postgraduate knowledge and skills in the workplace'.

HOW DO I BECOME A CRITICAL THINKER?

It seems likely that critical thinking is a learnable skill. Certainly the move of health professional education into the university setting and, more recently, the requirement for most health professional preparation programmes to be at graduate level appears to be an acknowledgement that critical thinking skills are both desirable for health professionals, but also will be more readily facilitated by degree level preparation.

It has also been suggested that it is the teaching style used in postgraduate education that helps in the transformation of learners from an unquestioning position to accepting the relativity of knowledge. Knight (1997), in his book on taught Master's degrees, makes the point that teaching methods must move away from didactic approaches associated with surface as opposed to deep learning in order to contribute 'to the learner, practitioner and professional autonomy' (Knight, 1997, p. 5). The student must be engaged in active learning such as applying, evaluating and communicating information in order to actively promote critical thinking skills.

Problem-based learning is increasingly used in the education of professionals in health and social care as a strategy for promoting critical thinking. Essentially, problem-based learning is a small-group teaching method that combines the acquisition of knowledge with the development of generic skills and attitudes. Educationally, it is theoretically grounded in adult learning theory and is predicted to produce a better learning environment and improved outcomes in terms of graduate knowledge, skills, and attitudes (Wood, 2008). You may find that assessments and classroom activities on your postgraduate course are often centred on real clinical issues and case studies for this reason.

However, exposure to higher education is clearly not the only vehicle for developing critical thinking. If we refer back to the work of Moon (2006, p. 109), she reported that Baxter Magolda (1996) found that two influences seemed to facilitate progress to the contextual knowing stage in students: firstly, exposure to the experience of postgraduate education, but also being placed in situations where they have to make significant decisions in their professional life, particularly those decisions that involved interactions with peers to explore and evaluate opinions. Taylor (2000, p. 74) proposes the use of a 'critical friend' to support practitioners by challenging attitudes and behaviours, assisting the practitioner to make sense of their practice and come to appropriate decisions.

This suggests the importance of both your academic studies and your professional experiences in the workplace in the development of your cognitive behaviours and critical thinking abilities.

ACTIVITY

List three activities that you could undertake in order to support the development of your critical thinking skills.

Some activities you might want to consider in developing your critical thinking skills are provided in Figure 4.

---

1. Identify a colleague on your course to pair up with so that you can act as 'critical friends' for each other and have a go at peer-reviewing each other's work prior to handing it in.

2. Form reading pairs to undertake critiques of papers and then share the findings.

3. Jointly construct notes after hearing a mini-lecture – share, compare and critique each other's ideas.

4. Get in the habit of asking yourself (or even better, jotting down) at the end of each lecture or learning activity – what new information have I gained? What are the implications of this for my developing understanding of this subject?

5. Start maintaining a reflective learning diary in which incidents or issues that occur in your academic or professional life are recorded and reflected upon.

Figure 4. *Some activities you might want to consider in developing your critical thinking skills*

The role of reflection

The role of reflection is widely cited in health literature as a process for learning from experience (Higher Education Academy, 2004). Boyd and Fales (1983) stated that reflection

> is the core difference between whether a person repeats the same experience several times becoming highly proficient at one behaviour, or learns from experience in such a way that he or she is cognitively or affectively changed.
>
> (Boyd and Fales, 1983, p. 38)

In other words, new understanding is developed by returning to an experience for a retrospective analysis, exploring the theory, knowledge and experience to understand it in a different way. Johns (1996) promotes reflection as a means by which the practitioner can:

> expose, confront and understand the contradictions between the way she or he practices and what is desirable … to empower the practitioner to take action to appropriately resolve these contradictions.
>
> (Johns, 1996, p. 1137)

Clearly what is being described here is a potential vehicle for both using and developing the skills underpinning critical thinking. Johns (1995) went on to describe the use of a model of guided reflection utilising cue questions or reflective cues to challenge the practitioner to explore all angles of a situation, and ultimately deepen and strengthen the reflective process. This is illustrated in Figure 5.

Johns' model aims to enable the practitioner to 'access, understand and learn through his or her lived experiences' (Johns, 1995, p. 226). The critical thinker will inevitably engage in critical reflection and this model provides a means of framing and guiding the analysis of practice. However, it is important to acknowledge that expert practitioners are likely to use the model flexibly as they integrate it into their own personal frameworks for learning from practice.

A full exploration of reflection is beyond the scope of this chapter and is available elsewhere. However, it is worth pointing out that the concept of reflection as a learning tool has not been without its critics (Mackintosh, 1998). Rolfe and Gardner (2006) report on the growing disquiet that reflection 'is at best a form of repressive self surveillance, and at worst a deliberate managerial strategy to produce docile and compliant workers' (Rolfe and Gardner, 2006, p. 594). However, they go on to suggest that if the focus of the reflection is primarily concerned with learning about professional practice, as opposed to learning about ourselves in a very personal way, then it offers the potential to empower individuals.

Write a description of the experience.

Aesthetics

What was I trying to achieve?

Why did I respond as I did?

What were the consequences of that for the patient? Others? Myself?

How was this person feeling (or those other people)?

How did I know that?

Personal

How did I feel in this situation?

What internal factors were influencing me?

Ethics

How did my actions match with my beliefs?

What factors made me act in incongruent ways?

Empirics

What knowledge did or should have informed me?

Reflexivity

How does this connect with previous experiences?

Could I handle this better in similar situations?

What would be the consequences of alternative actions for the patient/others/myself?

How do I NOW feel about this experience?

Can I support myself and others better as a consequence?

Has this experience changed my ways of knowing?

Figure 5. *Johns' model of structured reflection, 10th version (Johns, 1995)*

SUMMARY

This chapter has explored what is meant by critical thinking and considered the characteristics and skills that underpin the concept. In summary, we have suggested that critical reflection is purposeful and that it challenges assumptions, explores alternatives and differentiates between fact and opinion. It is associated with an understanding of the contextual nature of knowledge and the ability and orientation to question and critique. Critical thinking is therefore increasingly important for professionals in health and social care to make sense of and be responsive to the many challenges in the work environment.

Critical reflection	
Identify at least three things that you have learned from this chapter.	1. 2. 3.
How do you plan to use this knowledge?	1. 2. 3.
How will you evaluate the effectiveness of your plan?	1. 2. 3.
What further knowledge and evidence do you need?	1. 2. 3.

FURTHER READING

Moon, J. (2008) *Critical Thinking: An Exploration of Theory and Practice*. London: Routledge
This is an interesting book that explores the literature on critical thinking in a very readable way and, in particular, how it can be developed in students.

www.criticalthinking.org
This is a useful website entitled 'The critical thinking community'. It is an American website and contains a range of interesting resources and links to all aspects of critical thinking.

3

BECOMING AN INDEPENDENT LEARNER

This chapter covers the following key issues:

- the concept of independent learning in relation to Master's level study;
- the adult learner;
- self-motivation;
- managing your studies;
- the challenges faced by Master's students;
- identifying support;
- getting and making use of feedback;
- strategies to manage and support independent learning.

By the end of this chapter you should be able to:

- articulate your strengths and weaknesses in relation to planning and managing your studies;
- reflect on the importance of independent study within Master's level while also being aware of the support mechanisms that are available;
- discuss how you can effectively manage your studies and maximise your study opportunities.

INTRODUCTION

There are many different reasons why people choose to study for a Master's level qualification. For those working within health and social care, the potential to improve future employment prospects is often a key factor. However, health and social care professionals also have to meet their professional body's continuing professional development requirements in order to remain on their professional register and, within the context of lifelong learning, there is an acknowledgement that continued learning is valuable and is viewed as a means to improve the quality of care (DH, 2001). The knowledge and skills that you develop through undertaking this level of study will offer you the opportunity to consider your own practice area in some significant depth, while also further developing academic skills such as critical analytical skills and powers of reasoning. In addition, there are 'value-added' personal development skills to consider, such as the skills you develop and improve as you become an independent learner. For example, highly developed and finely tuned time management and prioritisation skills are clearly skills that you will utilise within your working environment. Indeed, Becker (2004, p. 42) goes further and lists a whole range of personal qualities that develop through studying at postgraduate level – qualities that an existing or potential employer may find desirable in an employee. These include:

- determination;
- the will to succeed;
- flexibility;
- curiosity;
- the ability to cope with change;
- self-discipline;
- analytical proficiency;
- self-motivation;
- thinking clearly;
- expressing yourself thoroughly;
- applying common sense to challenges.

As Becker (2004) states, many of these personal qualities may already be well developed and will continue to develop as you progress through your course. This chapter will assist you to consider how you might utilise this skills base to good effect in order to progress successfully through your studies. The activities will also allow you opportunity to reflect on which skills may require further development.

Master's level students 'are expected to have shown originality in the application of knowledge and in problem-solving and demonstrated understanding of how the boundaries of knowledge are advanced through research' (House, 2010). Developing your skills and knowledge to this extent requires a significant level of motivation and commitment. In addition, prior to commencing your Master's degree, you may have studied at undergraduate level and been significantly supported by lecturers to achieve your degree. Master's level study, as described in Chapter 1, focuses on you being a much more independent learner. This may feel a little daunting as traditional undergraduate teaching makes way for a programme of study that encourages self-management, self-reliance and the creation of new understanding and meaning (Garner and Wallace, 1997). This shift to higher-level thinking can cause some anxiety in students and there is often a fear of the unknown, of moving from undergraduate to postgraduate study and wondering what will be expected. In order to cope with this, it is important that you learn, from the outset, how to self-manage your studies effectively through facilitating and maximising your learning opportunities and prioritising tasks appropriately. This chapter will explore this in more detail and give advice on how best to manage and support your studies at Master's level.

THE ADULT LEARNER

It could be argued that Master's level study and the move towards being an independent learner is intrinsically linked with the concept of adult learning and the work of Malcolm Knowles (1990). Knowles defined 'andragogy' as the art and science of helping adults learn (as opposed to 'pedagogy', which is the art and science of teaching children) and he was one of the first to theorise adult learning as a self-directed inquiry process whereby adults take more control of their own learning within a co-operative, mutually trusting learning environment.

Knowles argues that there are certain assumptions relating to the characteristics of adult learners that differentiate them from child learners. The two models are based on different assumptions surrounding six key dimensions (Quinn and Hughes, 2007). These are:

- the learner's need to know;
- the learner's self-concept;
- the role of the learner's experience;
- the learner's readiness to learn;
- the learner's orientation to learning;
- the learner's motivation.

ACTIVITY

Consider how the above dimensions might relate specifically to the adult learner and give examples.

As part of the activity, and in view of your previous learning experiences, you may have considered the dimension of 'orientation to learning' and the extent to which the adult takes responsibility and control for their learning, perhaps through undertaking self-directed activities. It is interesting to further consider this in relation to the type of learning being undertaken by adults. For example, within a problem-solving approach to learning, there is an expectation that the learner will take a significant amount of responsibility. This approach is particularly appropriate for professionals working within health and social care in order to facilitate the application of theoretical concepts to practice. Burns (1995, p. 233) summarises this within the context of adult learning, stating:

> By adulthood people are self-directing. This is the concept that lies at the heart of andragogy ... andragogy is therefore student-centred, experience-based, problem-oriented and collaborative very much in the spirit of the humanist approach to learning and education ... the whole educational activity turns on the student.

ACTIVITY

At this point it would be useful for you to consider how andragogy may influence the approach your lecturers may take and what this will mean for you in terms of your responsibilities to engage as an adult learner.

Table 1 summarises the different assumptions on which pedagogy and andragogy are based.

Assumptions	Pedagogy	Andragogy
Learner's need to know.	Students must learn what they are taught in order to pass their tests.	Adults need to know why they must learn something.
Learner's self-concept.	Dependency: decisions about learning are controlled by teacher.	Self-direction: adults take responsibility for their own learning.
Role of learner's experience.	It is the teacher's experience that is seen as important. The learner's experience is seen as of little use as a learning resource.	Adults have greater, and more varied experience, which serves as a rich resource for learning.
Learner's readiness to learn.	Learner's readiness is dependent upon what the teacher wants the learner to learn.	Adult's readiness relates to the things he or she needs to know and do in real life.
Student's orientation to learning.	Learning equates with the subject matter/content of the curriculum.	Adults have a life-centred orientation to learning involving problem-solving and task-centred approaches.
Student's motivation.	Learner's motivation is from external sources such as teacher approval, grades and parental pressures.	Adult's motivation is largely internal, such as self-esteem, quality of life and job satisfaction.

Table 1. *The different assumptions of pedagogy and andragogy (Quinn and Hughes, 2007, p. 28)*

As you progress through your postgraduate studies and further develop your skills and knowledge, your learning will become increasingly independent and your reliance on lecturers will decrease. Your lecturers will take on a more facilitative role in your learning, providing guidance and support as and when you require it. With this in mind, it would be timely to consider the notion of andragogy and adult learning in relation to your own learning and your ability to succeed in your studies.

ACTIVITY

Consider the assumptions of adult learners in more detail. Consider how they might specifically relate to your studies at Master's level.

Through undertaking this activity you may have noticed how the assumptions can relate and interrelate with each other. For example, as you considered the 'learner's readiness to learn' and 'learner's motivation', this may have led you to consider the importance of being ready to learn the things you need to know. This frequently occurs in relation to successfully fulfilling a role or job requirement. Clearly this is also of importance to professionals working within health and social care where further study at Master's level may allow you to broaden and deepen your knowledge in relation to your practice and ultimately increase your job satisfaction.

The assertions regarding adult learning and the claims of such a stark difference between andragogy and pedagogy have been the subject of some debate (Davenport, 1993; Tennant, 1996) and it is evident that either or both approaches may be appropriate at different times depending on learner need. However, the characteristics of adult learners support the move from what may be viewed as a predominantly pedagogical approach within undergraduate study to the more independently focused learning that is expected within Master's study. Knowles' assumptions focus on the increasingly independent nature of adult learning which supports many of the aims of Master's level study.

BECOMING A MASTER'S STUDENT

As has previously been stated, there is an increased requirement at Master's level for you to become an independent learner and not to rely solely on lectures or lecturers for your information. Studying at Master's level requires an element of transition as you to take responsibility for your learning – this includes motivating yourself and managing your studies and your workload.

Making the transition from undergraduate to postgraduate study has not been widely acknowledged within the literature. This may be due to an assumption that the transition is unproblematic as a result of the majority of postgraduate students having some level of existing knowledge and experience of study. As Tobbell, O'Donnell and Zammit (2008) acknowledge, the literature relating to transition has argued that students' existing knowledge is simply relocated in a new context. While it is clear that you will probably have developed some skills and knowledge through previous study, the extent to which these skills are current and up to date depends on the length of time since you last studied.

ACTIVITY

List the key skills you developed while studying as an undergraduate or within a professional development course. Do you feel these skills remain current as you commence your new course?

You may have identified skills such as reading, articulating your ideas and planning and writing essays. These are all transferable skills that you will continue to utilise and further develop as you progress with your studies. However, other skills relating to prioritising tasks and time management may not have been viewed with such importance at undergraduate level and it is these skills that you will need to focus on, from the start, if you are to be successful at Master's level. A study conducted by Tobbell *et al.* (2008) concluded that postgraduate students sometimes had difficulty in becoming independent learners because of limited available assistance. Therefore, you should consider in some depth your current skills, any gaps in terms of your study skills and what you need to do to develop these skills further.

Self-motivation

As has already been discussed, studying at Master's level is significantly different from undergraduate level and requires a much greater degree of self-discipline. There is an expectation that your learning will be more independent and your tutors will provide focus and support with your studies rather than be providers of all knowledge. Therefore, it is clear that you will require a high level of motivation to assist with your studies as you negotiate getting the balance right between studying and the other demands on your time.

ACTIVITY

What are your key motivating factors for undertaking your Master's course?

Your considerations will be personal to you and your future aspirations, be they work-related or for personal fulfilment. You will need to keep these motivations in mind as you progress through your course. Motivation and, in particular, self-motivation, is an important requirement in the successful pursuit of a goal. Identifying and understanding your motivating factors and the benefits a Master's award will bring will assist you to successfully complete the course.

Lieb (1991) described six motivating factors for adult learning that you may wish to use and further consider in relation to your personal motivation.

- **Social relationships**: to make new friends, to meet a need for associations and friendships.
- **External expectations**: to comply with instructions from someone else; to fulfil the expectations or recommendations of someone with formal authority.
- **Social welfare**: to improve ability to serve mankind, prepare for service to the community, and improve ability to participate in community work.
- **Personal advancement**: to achieve higher status in a job, secure professional advancement, and stay abreast of competitors.
- **Escape/stimulation**: to relieve boredom, provide a break in the routine of home or work, and provide a contrast to other exacting details of life.
- **Cognitive interest**: to learn for the sake of learning, seek knowledge for its own sake, and to satisfy an inquiring mind.

(Lieb, 1991)

ACTIVITY

Consider these factors in more depth in relation to your personal motivation. Place them in order of priority and importance to you.

As Master's level study requires you to be much more independent than undergraduate study, you do need to be aware that you will be working by yourself for much of the time. With this in mind, you need to consider your self-motivation in relation to this, otherwise you could end up feeling a little isolated and unfocused as your studies progress. In particular, this could be the case if a significant element of the course is studied by distance learning or online. Regardless of the mode of study, there will be support available but, at postgraduate level, this may not be as visible as when you studied previously.

While it is important to consider the positive aspects regarding successful completion of your course, it is also essential to consider the issues that may have an impact on your ability to study effectively. Tobbell *et al.* (2008) identified that postgraduate level students had complex personal lives where there was a fine balance between work, family and study. These factors should all be considered and it has been acknowledged that achieving a balance takes time and is not easy (Tobbell *et al.*, 2008).

It is also essential that you consider the negative aspects that may hinder or distract you from your studies. Utilising the SWOT analysis tool will assist you to identify your strengths and weaknesses, but will also enable you to understand more clearly the areas you need to focus upon, and perhaps develop, in order to successfully complete your studies.

SWOT analysis

The SWOT analysis (see Figure 1) is a strategic development tool (Morrison, 2006) that can be utilised, for example in business and higher education, to identify key issues and possible opportunities while, at the same time, identifying how weaknesses may be focused upon and eliminated.

Figure 1. *The SWOT matrix model (Morrison, 2006)*

- Strengths: attributes that are helpful to achieving the objective.
- Weaknesses: attributes that may be harmful or might hinder achieving the objective.
- Opportunities: external conditions that are helpful to achieving the objective.
- Threats: external conditions which could potentially cause damage to the objective.

ACTIVITY

Divide a blank page into four quarters. In each quarter, consider one of:

- your strengths in terms of your learning;
- your weaknesses in terms of your learning;
- any opportunities as a result of your learning;
- any threats to your learning.

You may have considered some of the following or wish to use the ideas presented below to help guide your thinking.

- **Your strengths** – for example, your unique abilities, existing skills and knowledge, etc.
- **Your weaknesses** – some potential areas for personal development such as, for example, the need to identify your support network.
- **Opportunities** – possibilities for career development that you could take advantage of once you have successfully achieved your Master's degree.
- **Threats to the successful completion of your degree** – in the external environment, that may be outside your control, that you should take into account. For example, work and/ or family commitments, etc.

After completing your SWOT analysis, it is vital that you learn from the activity in order to build on your strengths and plan to reduce your weaknesses. You should now be able to consider how to utilise your strengths to their full potential, while addressing your weaknesses through identifying and making changes to overcome them. Through doing this you will be able to maximise your ability to succeed in your studies.

ACTIVITY

How will you ensure that you:

- maximise your strengths and any opportunities;
- develop your skills and knowledge in relation to your weaknesses;
- overcome any threats?

Having a proactive approach will allow you to put plans in place to address any weaknesses or threats as they arise, while also allowing you to acknowledge your strengths and opportunities. The basic SWOT analysis allows you to consider the four areas in relative isolation. However, a key benefit of the completed process is that it also provides an overview of everything in each individual area in relation to all the other areas. For example, in order to take advantage of an opportunity you may need to address an area of weakness. It is also important to remember to perform a SWOT analysis on a regular basis as your skills, knowledge, and indeed environment, may change as you progress on your course.

The advantages of undertaking a SWOT analysis are that:

- it is a simple tool that requires only the cost of time to do;
- it can assist you to focus on potential problem areas, while also supporting the generation of new ideas to help support your studies as you identify your particular strengths;
- as you become more aware of the potential threats to your studies, you can plan accordingly and counteract them when they happen.

There are also some disadvantages of SWOT analysis. There is a potential to generalise and simply compile lists rather than be specific about issues. It is therefore important that you consider the issues you identify in greater detail and in relation to each other to ensure that effective strategies can be planned.

MANAGING YOUR STUDIES

Undertaking study at Master's level is a varied experience. Depending on the type of course you have enrolled on, you may be attending lectures, seminars, group or individual tutorials and supervisory sessions. You will be faced with a vast array of varying views and perspectives from a number of different lecturers, while being required to determine your own opinions and ideas through undertaking independent study or research modules. This can feel confusing at first so it is essential that, from an early stage, you develop the skills to manage your studies. Race (2007) identifies a number of characteristics associated with independent learning. They are:

- working through learning resource materials;
- freedom to work at one's own pace;
- freedom to work at a chosen time;
- freedom to work at an alternative location.

Race (2007) also identifies a further characteristic that relates to the freedom to fail to undertake any of the above. This acknowledges the nature and one of the potential dangers of independent study when there is no one monitoring progress except you. Managing your studies and your course effectively will assist you to make sense of all this and will allow you to keep the overall aim of the course in mind as you successfully achieve the required learning outcomes for specific modules.

Creating a study environment

The need to identify some space for study is a priority and this should be sought and negotiated, if required, prior to commencing your course. If possible, some dedicated space that is yours alone should be sought – a place where you can work uninterrupted with no distractions. You will need computer access and computer availability at times that suit you. Competing with other family members for computer access has been acknowledged within the literature as being problematic and frustrating for students undertaking e-learning courses (McVeigh, 2008). Pre-empting this with appropriate planning and negotiation should ease the potentially stressful situation.

ACTIVITY

Consider other things you will need within your study environment that will allow you to manage your studies effectively.

You may have considered, among other things, the need to ensure adequate shelving or storage for books, journals and files. Managing the information you collect and generate will be key to your success and you will need to ensure adequate space is available to store resources as you progress through your course.

The importance of learning support

Identifying at an early stage the type of support and guidance you might require will assist you more easily to realise when support is needed. Pre-empting the need for support will ensure that you are able to identify and seek support at an early stage rather than risk the possibility of becoming unfocused and demoralised with your studies. It is important to avoid this. A study conducted by Richardson *et al.* (2007) compared academic approaches to study by students on a Master's programme and an undergraduate programme. The results identified that Master's students were less confident than undergraduates in relation to having clear goals and standards.

While the research was focused on a particular programme of study, it is clear that this could be relevant to any Master's student in view of the decreasing reliance on lecturers and the move towards independence at this level of study. Therefore, the need to acknowledge and address problems before they become too big is imperative. Taking this proactive approach is an indication of a well-motivated student.

ACTIVITY

Consider some areas where you think you might need assistance with your studies and identify where the support might come from.

The type of areas you may have considered in terms of requiring assistance may have included, for example, help with planning and writing essays and reports, understanding new concepts, identifying and locating key literature or other materials. The support you identified in relation to these may have included a combination of face-to-face and online support from both lecturers/research supervisors and library staff, which is completely appropriate. You should also not underestimate the value and vast amount of support you can receive from your fellow students, many of whom will be facing similar issues and challenges as they undertake postgraduate study.

Peer support

Becker (2004) suggests that early, proactive identification and creation of a peer support group can reduce the isolation some students feel when studying at postgraduate level. She identifies that meeting regularly with peers, perhaps initially from a good seminar group, can support you as you are able to discuss work and workloads together. In addition, Becker (2004) also suggests that keeping family and friends regularly informed of progress or otherwise can assist when you face challenging times. Race (2007) identifies several points as important in relation to peer support, namely:

- realising how much you deepen your learning every time you explain something to a fellow student;

- valuing what they know and not making them feel small with what you know and what they don't;
- recognising their abilities and expertise;
- being open and sharing information with them.

These points are clearly important in developing and maintaining good relationships with your fellow students regardless of whether you are undertaking a taught face-to-face course or studying through distance learning.

ACTIVITY

Race (2007, p. 114) has developed the exercise listed in Table 2 below that allows you to consider your current approaches to working with other students and identifies areas of focus where you may wish to further develop relationships in order to be more effective.

Approaches to working with fellow students	Very like me	Quite like me	Not like me
I find it really useful to work with fellow students and do so in many aspects of my course.			
I set up my own ways of working with fellow students, such as study syndicates.			
I like working with fellow students, but I'm easily distracted and my productivity falls too much.			
I don't really like working with fellow students as they slow me down too much.			
Why should I work with fellow students? I'm competing against them!			
I find it really valuable to explain things to fellow students; this helps me to learn them better myself.			
I find it very useful to have things explained to me by fellow students; I can often understand them better than my lecturers.			

I find that there are a few fellow students that I can really open up to and with whom I can openly share my feelings and views.			
I don't work much with fellow students as when I try to they only make me more anxious about my own studying.			
I just don't seem to find the right sorts of fellow students with whom to get down to some useful studying.			

Table 2. *Making the most of your fellow students (Race, 2007)*

Having undertaken this activity, you will now be able to identify more clearly your strengths and weaknesses in this area and also be able to identify areas that you may need to develop further in order to fully engage with your fellow students and optimise the support you could receive.

Support from family, friends and colleagues

Studying at Master's level will involve a significant investment in terms of your personal life as, prior to commencing your studies, you may already be juggling work commitments with responsibilities such as caring for children and/or elderly parents, and also have other interests (Gatrell, 2006). Your studies will inevitably have some impact on the amount of personal time you have available and there will be some displacement in terms of the contributions of care you can make to family or friends (Price, 2004). Therefore, it is essential that you discuss this with close family members and friends and seek their support – this will prove invaluable as you commence and progress your studies.

The importance of this more informal support is acknowledged within the literature. A study conducted by Gopee (2002) concluded that professional learning can be enhanced through social contacts from non-healthcare acquaintances. Practical offers of help with chores, ongoing support and encouragement, and negotiating appropriate time and opportunity to study were cited by participants as being particularly helpful. Price (2004) conducted a study that described and acknowledged the importance of 'lay supporters' and the contribution they made to successful student progress. The study identified that students negotiated 'relief duties' such as asking family and friends to take over, for example, tasks and chores, and 'protection duties' whereby lay supporters assisted participants to study by deflecting commitments or appointments with others until after assignment deadlines had been met. It is therefore evident that family attitudes can have a significant impact on a student's motivation and practical ability to study effectively. It would be useful for you to reflect upon this further in relation to your own circumstances.

ACTIVITY

Identify your key responsibilities within your personal life. Consider how your studies might impact on these, and when and how you might seek support from your family and friends when your studies need to be prioritised when, for example, you have an assignment deadline to meet.

You may have considered the regular times you spend with family and friends, perhaps at weekends, doing activities you enjoy. There is no doubt that, at some point, your studies will have some impact on your ability to devote as much time to family and leisure activities, however much you feel you would like to continue as normal. If you have not discussed this prior to considering or commencing your course, it is understandable that family and friends may feel unsympathetic and a little disgruntled as you prioritise your time towards your studies. Considering these types of issues prior to commencing your studies will assist you to plan and negotiate the times when you need to study, while still maintaining some quality time with family and friends when you may not have assignment deadlines looming.

Support from your employer and colleagues

In addition to support from family and friends, you will need to consider the impact your studies may have on your professional working life and how this may affect your ability to achieve a good work–life balance. You may be able to negotiate some study leave with your employer, either on a regular basis or when you are facing an assignment deadline. If not, it may be that you can arrange to take some annual leave when you know you will be under pressure to complete your academic work. Having a flexible approach and being able to negotiate time away from work that will suit all parties may facilitate some success. You should keep your line manager and colleagues informed of your studies and you should utilise available opportunities to discuss your academic work and its application to practice with work colleagues. Their support and the discussions you generate will assist you in developing discussions and ideas and this will also allow you to demonstrate the work applicability of your studies.

Lay supporters and critical readers

A study conducted by Price (2004) describes the important role lay supporters play in supporting students and discusses the notion of a 'critical reader' as a key means of support.

While participants in this study sought critical readers or lay reviewers to 'comment upon the written expression of ideas' (p. 17) rather than the subject content, it is clear that having one or more critical readers from a similar professional background could offer you considerable support and contribution to your studies.

Discussing issues relating to support in detail can be quite daunting and difficult prior to commencing your course, when you may not have a true idea of timetables, workload, assignment deadlines, etc. However, ultimately you will have to accept that your course will generate a significant workload that must be managed if you are to be successful. Gatrell (2006, p. 53) states that 'most students will need to spend an average of 10–12 hours per week on part-time study (especially if they are working at postgraduate level)'. The consequences of finding this time should not be underestimated and the sacrifices you make to successfully gain a Master's degree will also be experienced to some extent by those close to you. Careful planning and acknowledgment by all involved that compromises will need to be made will help to minimise the impact of your studies while ensuring optimum conditions to enable you to succeed.

Lecturer support and making the most of your feedback

The support that your lecturers can offer through face-to-face, telephone or online tutorials is crucial to your success. There is a need for you to identify where your tutorial support and your feedback are going to come from and to access these on a regular basis. If you are undertaking a distance learning course you should access the forums and chat rooms where key topics and issues can be discussed, often with both fellow students and lecturers.

Many of your lecturers on professionally focused health and social care courses will be experienced professionals who have also encountered the difficulties of undertaking part-time study while holding down a full-time or part-time job. They will therefore have some understanding of the personal and practical challenges you will encounter from time to time and be able to offer support, assistance and practical guidance to help you to succeed.

As already discussed and acknowledged, part-time students have significant demands on their time (Garner and Wallace, 1997; Gatrell, 2006). These demands can impact on study time with only limited time available to reflect and get to grips with the understanding of new concepts. Garner and Wallace (1997) report that students, when under time constraint pressures, tend to become task orientated and concentrate on 'doing the reading' or 'getting the essay written' (Garner and Wallace, 1997, p. 56), regardless of whether learning and understanding have taken place. As already identified, at Master's level there is an expectation that you will extend your depth of knowledge through consideration and understanding of increasingly complex concepts (House, 2010). You will not be able to do this without having the time and space to attend lectures, tutorials and supervision sessions with your lecturers. Attempts to learn through a task-orientated model or the 'rote-learning' route as identified by Garner and Wallace (1997) will result in failure as these techniques will not allow you to develop sufficient depth of understanding to successfully meet the assessment requirements at Master's level.

Receiving feedback

Depending on the type of course you are undertaking, you may, if on a taught Master's, most frequently see lecturers during lectures as part of a large group. These encounters, while important for your learning, will offer you little in terms of the support requirements and feedback that are personal to you. Arranging to meet a lecturer or supervisor on a one-to-one basis will allow you the opportunity to discuss your individual needs in more depth and to explore issues that are of concern. It is also particularly important that you consider the value of receiving feedback within this context.

ACTIVITY

What kind of feedback might you experience or expect to receive at Master's level?

Getting sufficient feedback that allows you to chart your progress can be viewed as a supportive mechanism, whether the feedback is positive or more critical. The need to monitor your own work and progress is an essential component of independent learning and therefore the feedback you receive should be viewed as feedback for your learning rather than feedback of your learning. This means that you should proactively use the comments you receive from lecturers to further develop and improve your skills and knowledge. This will allow you to focus on areas that require further development, while acknowledging the areas that are progressing well. This provides you with focus and ensures that you know how you are progressing through the course – and, of course, this is a huge motivational factor if things are going well.

ACTIVITY

How might you prepare for a one-to-one meeting with a lecturer? What would be useful for you to consider prior to attending the meeting?

One-to-one meetings can feel quite daunting and intimidating initially. Using these meetings effectively involves some thought and planning prior to attending. Writing down questions and possible ideas beforehand will help you to focus on the areas of greatest concern and will allow you the opportunity to take some control of the situation so that you are able to achieve your aims for the meeting. Race (2007) also suggests that preparing and sending questions in advance of the meeting allows the lecturer to prepare more thoroughly. If you are undertaking a distance learning course, the same principles will apply even if you are unable to meet face-to-face. Good preparation before an online tutorial will allow you to use the time effectively in order to enhance your studies. Race (2007, p. 82) identifies some good habits within a one-to-one context, namely:

- valuing, seeking and using one-to-one opportunities;
- listening well and capturing the scene;
- radiating interest and enthusiasm;
- seeing one-to-one contexts as opportunities to develop a partnership.

The final point seems particularly apt for Master's level students who, by the very nature of their studies, are working much more independently and therefore need to develop and maintain good networks where support, when required, can be easily accessed.

Library/information technology support

The university library will be a key resource where you will find a range of services to support your studies. Support teams within the library work closely with lecturers and researchers to provide appropriate information resources that meet the requirements of learning, teaching and research activities throughout the university.

ACTIVITY

List the range of services that you would expect to find in your university library that would support your studies.

You may have included services such as flexible access and opening times. Some university libraries are now open 24 hours a day, seven days a week, which may be significant if you are working shifts, extra hours, etc., and require access out of normal working hours. Specialist subject area librarians will usually be available to offer you specific advice and assistance. You may also have considered services such as:

- access to information databases;
- journals;
- newspapers;
- general reference sources;
- inter-library loan services;
- printing/photocopying services;
- IT support;
- study skills support;
- support with using the library.

Many resources will be available online, which should assist you to manage your study time more effectively. You will, however, need to consider your skills and knowledge relating to computer literacy in order to take full advantage of the range of online services.

In addition, one aspect of Master's level study that is worthy of some further consideration is the use of the virtual learning environment (VLE). Virtual learning environments are being used increasingly often within higher education, and particularly within Master's level study where self-directed learning and independent study are encouraged. Depending on the type of course you are undertaking, you may study entire modules online or access directed learning activities, information and resources as part of a taught module. The support you receive and the way this will be provided will be determined by the type of course you are undertaking but library staff will be well equipped to deal with particular concerns relating to this mode of delivery. As a result of the increasing use of digital technological tools to support learning and teaching on Master's courses, you will need to self-assess your computer skills and identify any areas that will require further development.

ACTIVITY

Consider your information technology (IT) skills. Identify any skills deficits and identify where you will seek specific support to address these.

You may have identified that you require support with searching the online databases. This area may well be addressed within an induction programme but, if not or you require additional one-to-one support, you should contact your librarian for advice. You should seek out the names and contact numbers of key library personnel to ensure that you are easily able to contact them should problems arise.

Librarians and other learning support staff are rich sources of information and you should ensure that you take advantage of their vast experience and knowledge in order to optimise your studies and make best use of your study time. It is usual to require help with accessing library resources, and perhaps even more so at Master's level as you search for more obscure literature in order to expand the boundaries of your knowledge.

SUMMARY

This chapter has explored some of the challenges faced by Master's students as they juggle demanding professional and personal lives with ongoing study requirements. Independent learning has been identified as a key requirement of Master's level study and therefore strategies have been suggested in order to facilitate the identification and development of appropriate skills that will encourage and support independent learning. Support mechanisms have been identified and discussed and key resources have been identified to maximise study opportunities in order to facilitate success at Master's level.

Critical reflection	
Identify at least three things that you have learned from this chapter.	1. 2. 3.
How do you plan to use this knowledge?	1. 2. 3.
How will you evaluate the effectiveness of your plan?	1. 2. 3.
What further knowledge and evidence do you need?	1. 2. 3.

FURTHER READING

Becker, L. (2004) *How to Manage Your Postgraduate Course*. Basingstoke: Palgrave Macmillan
This book focuses on the management of the processes involved in gaining a postgraduate qualification and offers practical advice and guidance on a range of key issues.

Cottrell, S. (2008) *The Study Skills Handbook*. Basingstoke: Palgrave Macmillan
This is a useful book that gives many specific and detailed exercises to facilitate the development of key study skills.

Gatrell, C. (2006) *Managing Part-time Study*. Maidenhead: Open University Press
This is an interesting book that explores in some depth the unique challenges facing part-time students. The book offers advice and is illustrated with real-life case studies.

Race, P. (2007) *How to Get a Good Degree* (2nd Ed.). Maidenhead: Open University Press. This book aims to help students to achieve their full potential as they study for a degree. Many useful exercises and tasks are presented that will assist students in identifying strengths and areas for further development.

4

FINDING AND CRITIQUING LITERATURE

This chapter covers the following key issues:

- reading as a postgraduate skill;
- literature searching;
- note-taking skills;
- avoiding plagiarism;
- critical appraisal skills.

By the end of this chapter you should be able to:

- discuss the importance of reading for Master's level students;
- undertake a literature search using academic information databases;
- demonstrate an awareness of how to avoid plagiarism by meticulous note-taking and sourcing all information carefully;
- critically appraise literature for relevance and quality.

INTRODUCTION

If we return to Chapter 2, you will see that one of the key outcomes of postgraduate study is the development of critical thinking skills. The critical thinker demonstrates the ability to interpret, analyse, evaluate and explain. In academic study, this involves interrogating the current state of knowledge on a subject. In this way the student gains 'mastery' or a critical understanding of a particular field or topic. This can only be achieved and demonstrated through the use of literature. This chapter will therefore explore how the postgraduate student can retrieve, critique and develop strategies for managing and utilising high-quality literature in academic work.

READING AS A POSTGRADUATE SKILL

Before we look at the process of finding high-quality information, it is worth considering the skills of reading in a more general sense.

What do we mean by 'reading in the academic sense', and what is the value of reading for the postgraduate student?

Reading is clearly more than just the recognition of words or phrases. It has been described as a process of constructing meaning by interacting with the text (Chandler, 1995). As we read, we use our prior knowledge along with clues from the text to construct meaning. Readers draw upon past experiences and prior knowledge to make inferences, evaluate validity and significance, and consider implications. Chandler (1995) also emphasises that, therefore, reading is not passive 'knowledge retrieval' and a text does not necessarily have one universal meaning for all readers. Indeed, readers may return to a specific article or textbook and reinterpret it in the light of further research.

Therefore, the value of reading is not just about finding out information, but is much more aligned to Moon's premise (discussed in detail in Chapter 2) that the critical thinker understands that all knowledge is contextual (Moon, 2008, p. 103). It will have different meanings depending on how, when and to what the knowledge is applied. The real value of reading is in interpreting and making sense of the text and applying it to a particular context.

In January 2008, in a speech to her supporters as a candidate for US president, Hillary Clinton was reported as saying 'I listened to you and in the process, I found my own voice' (Hillary Clinton, reported in *Guardian* newspaper, 9 January 2008). Postgraduate students may be encouraged by their lecturers to 'find their own voice'.

What does 'finding your own voice' mean in academic terms?

The Hillary Clinton quote is a good analogy for what Master's level students should be aiming for by engaging in wide reading around their topic – listening to the theoretical positions and views of others and, through the process of considering and reflecting upon their work, developing their own perspective. At undergraduate level, students may be criticised in their academic work for stating their own opinions on an issue without underpinning those opinions with a clear rationale derived from robust evidence. At postgraduate level, as you develop mastery of your subject, there is an expectation that you will develop and assert opinions by, for example, challenging conventional wisdom by critiquing seminal texts or concepts. The confidence and ability to do this is gained through the process of reading widely and assimilating the different literature within a discipline. Therefore, reading by students only has value if it can be applied by the student and is used to inform and develop their own ideas, thinking and, ultimately, for the health or social care professional, their practice.

ACTIVITY

What does 'reading widely' suggest to you?

Wide reading suggests that the thinking of a student, demonstrated in both discussions and in written assignments, has been informed by a good range of sources that reflect current knowledge of the subject. This could include:

- key textbooks;
- research articles;
- policy documents;
- local and national guidelines;
- expert opinion.

It also implies an obligation to keep up to date generally within your own discipline.

ACTIVITY

How do you keep up to date within your own discipline? What resources do you need to access on a regular basis to enable your professional knowledge within your specialty to be current?

You might have considered issues such as accessing a peer-reviewed professional journal regularly. This does not necessarily involve subscribing. Almost certainly your university library will have electronic access to key health and social care journals that you can access free of charge. Your union or professional body may also have free access to electronic journals. For example, the Royal College of Nursing has a range of full text journals and books available electronically to its members. It might also be useful to regularly check some key websites like, for example, the Department of Health website. Saving them on your personal computer under 'Favourites' will allow you to quickly check what is new in terms of publications.

Reading 'widely' also implies that the sources used have currency, relevance and have been subject to critical appraisal to ensure any findings are robust. We will return to these qualities in the section on critical appraisal of literature.

Strategic reading

It is worth mentioning here the concept of 'strategic reading'. In order to understand what is meant by this, we need to understand 'strategic learning'. Atherton (2009) discusses the differences between deep and surface learning. He stresses that these are not attributes of individuals, but approaches to learning that students may use. Figure 1 describes the characteristics of deep and surface learning.

Deep learning	Surface learning
Focus is on what is significant.	Focus is on the 'signs' (or on the learning as a signifier of something else).
Relates previous knowledge to new knowledge.	Focus is on unrelated parts of the task.
Relates knowledge from different courses.	Information for assessment is simply memorised.
Relates theoretical ideas to everyday experience.	Facts and concepts are associated unreflectively.
Relates and distinguishes evidence and argument.	Principles are not distinguished from examples.
Organises and structures content into coherent whole.	A task is treated as an external imposition.
Emphasis is internal, from within the student.	Emphasis is external, from demands of assessment.

Figure 1. *The characteristics of deep and surface learning (adapted from Atherton, 2009)*

As can be seen from Figure 1, the learning undertaken in surface learning is unlikely to be the embedded learning associated with the critical thinker, but is very superficial learning achieved for a specific outcome. Atherton suggests that surface learners who, for example, learn just enough to achieve good marks in an assessment, can be identified as 'strategic learners'. This is clearly not desirable for students who are aiming to demonstrate mastery of a subject through their postgraduate studies.

The concept of strategic learning can perhaps also be applied to students' reading habits.

ACTIVITY

Consider your reading habits.
- To what extent do you read in order to facilitate your learning in the widest sense?
- Do you only read 'strategically', i.e. when you have an assignment or piece of work to undertake, do you limit the scope of your reading to those sources that you can use within your assignment?

A postgraduate student who focuses only on achieving just enough 'strategic reading' to pass assignments is unlikely to maximise his or her academic potential, or indeed to really engage in a meaningful way in the advancement of knowledge and understanding in his or her specialty – as outlined in the learning outcomes for postgraduate study (QAA, 2008) discussed in Chapter 1. What is needed is focused reading – wide reading around the topic.

RETRIEVING RELEVANT CURRENT LITERATURE

There are thousands of health and social care journals published annually. Given, therefore, the vast range of literature in these disciplines it is essential that students develop strategies to be both time-efficient and effective in their search for robust information.

As discussed in Chapter 3, your university library or learning centre will be able to support you not just in accessing textbooks, but also with the process of literature searching. Indeed, most librarians or learning support staff will offer you introductory teaching sessions on using the library and searching for electronic and hard literature. The full process of literature retrieval is therefore not included in this chapter, but an overview of the key elements of undertaking a search is provided.

ACTIVITY

Spend a few minutes defining what is meant by the terms:

- a literature search;
- a literature review?

A literature search is a systematic and comprehensive search for published material on a specific topic. Once a literature search is undertaken, a review of the findings can be written up. This is known as a literature review and will usually include:

- an introduction and rationale for the topic reviewed;
- the search strategy used – databases searched, search terms used, any limits to the search such as UK journals only or date limits;
- a summary of the results – the number and type of articles/papers retrieved;
- a critical review of the literature identifying key themes or findings;
- a conclusion discussing the implications;
- a critique of the review – any limitations to the search, such as an inability to access certain papers.

An in-depth guide to undertaking a literature review can be found in Aveyard's book on the subject (Aveyard, 2009) – see further reading at the end of the chapter.

Do you know how to undertake a literature search using electronic information sources? Even if you have used the skills of literature searching in the past, it might be worth refreshing your skills. If not, find out what support is available to you from your university library or study support services.

Literature searching

There are five fundamental steps to undertaking a literature search. These are:

1. identify the focus of your search;
2. undertake a step-by-step search for the best evidence;
3. obtain copies of the appropriate literature generated by the search;
4. critically appraise the evidence in the literature;
5. apply the key findings in your work.

1. Identify the focus of your search

The first step is to recognise your information needs and to convert them into search terms. This is the starting point for planning your 'search strategy' – a considered plan to systematically search for relevant information. Search terms are generated from either a specific question to which you are seeking the answer such as, for example, 'what is the evidence that cognitive behaviour therapy is an effective treatment in the treatment of clinical depression?' Alternatively, you may not have a defined question at this stage and may want to review the evidence on a particular topic in order to understand a current issue in depth in that particular field such as, for example, hand washing and hospital-acquired infections.

Brainstorming or using a mind-map to consider different aspects of the topic that you could potentially review may help you to refine your topic area and identify more focused areas for your search. Figure 2 provides an example of the outcomes of such an exercise.

Hand washing and compliance by nursing and medical staff.
Hand washing and compliance by patients.
Hand washing and specific infections.
Hand washing and specific patient groups or specialties.
Hand washing education – what works in improving practice.
Hand washing techniques.
Use of hand washing lotions/hand rubs/alcohol rubs.
Hand washing and skin damage.

Figure 2. *A brainstorm on hand washing and infection control*

This brainstorm can then be used to create a list of key words and synonyms or similar terms. This is essential if you are going to effectively search the literature for relevant material.

2. Undertake a step-by-step search for the best evidence

Once you have identified your search terms, you are ready to search for literature. The most effective way to search for current best evidence on any topic is to undertake a literature search using one of the clinical knowledge databases (also known as information databases) available electronically via your university library. Your university library will give you full details of the available and relevant databases for your specialty. You can usually access university databases from your work or home computers as well as in the library premises.

What are information databases?

Information databases allow you to search electronically across a large number of journals, using keywords (search terms) to find articles on a topic you are interested in. For each subject area, e.g. nursing, midwifery, social work, there are usually several relevant databases. A small number of the many databases available for retrieving health and social care literature are described in Figure 3.

ASSIA (Applied social science index and abstracts)
Literature on social sciences, economics, employment, politics, race relations, health, education and crime. Mainly British journals.

CINAHL (Cumulative Index to Nursing and Allied Health Literature)
Literature on nursing, nutrition, dietetics, occupational therapy, rehabilitation and speech and language – some international journals included.

ChildData
Extensive database of resources for education, health and welfare of children and young people.

PsycINFO
International literature (including articles and book chapters) in psychology and related disciplines such as education, nursing social work and medicine.

Figure 3. *A selection of useful information databases for health and social care students*

Each database is created by a team of indexers who look through a prescribed set of journals, pulling out the key information from the articles within them, which they then include in the database. The databases usually provide the reference and abstract (short summary) of any article included. They will also link to the full text of the article so you can immediately access it if it is a free journal or if it is subscribed to by the university or organisation whose library facilities you are using to accessing the database.

A particularly useful database is the Cochrane library (**www.cochrane. co.uk/en/index. html**). This is a free, full text database of high-quality independent evidence on health care interventions. It includes systematic reviews from around the world. A systematic review is a summary of the best available evidence on a topic. A key feature is that the reviewers have followed a strict protocol to ensure that the review process is undertaken in a systematic way to identify, appraise and synthesise the relevant studies to find an answer to a specific question (Aveyard, 2009). Because of their rigorous nature, systematic reviews are therefore considered to be the 'gold standard' in terms of assessing quality of evidence on a topic. For example, the National Institute for Health and Clinical Excellence (NICE) uses systematic reviews to ensure its clinical guidelines are based on the best available evidence. However, it is important to note that the conclusion of a systematic review may be that there is an absence of solid evidence to reach a conclusion on the effectiveness of a particular intervention and that therefore may indicate the need for further research.

To undertake a search using an information database requires you to do the following.

- **Select the database or databases**. Ask your librarian for advice if you are unsure which databases are likely to yield the best information for your search terms.
- **Input your search term or terms**. You do not need to separate out words that are branches of the same word, as electronic databases have the facility to 'truncate' search terms. 'Truncate' means finding the base of a word to find any words that begin with that base like, for example, Nurs*, which will generate any articles with nurse, nurses, nursing in the title (Harvard, 2007).
- **Put limits on your search**. You need to decide how widely you will search. This is also known as setting your inclusion and exclusion criteria – what you choose to include and what you will omit from your search. For example, you might want to include a time limit, such as only articles published in the last five years. You may also wish to restrict the articles you retrieve to those published in British journals, as opposed to including the international literature. You may also decide to restrict your literature search to retrieving articles from full text journals only. This might be done for pragmatic reasons such as a lack of time and ease of access. However, you need to be aware that there may be crucial evidence that you may miss from journals that your university or library does not purchase as full text electronically. A systematic review of the literature on a topic would, of course, need to include all available literature, rather than a selective review.
- **Combine parts of a search**. When you conduct a search you will, in effect, carry out lots of small searches and put them together. Databases allow you to do this using the 'operator terms' OR and AND. If you are not familiar with this technique it is worth getting some training in literature searching to maximise the use of your time and effort.

- **Select the articles that look as if they might be useful**. This can be done initially by reading the abstract of the article or by skimming through the article on the screen to get a sense of whether it is focused on an area of relevance.

You need to ensure that you keep a record of your search strategy. You may return to it later on in your studies and want to add to and update it. Remember that your search strategy may develop as your search is under way. If, for example, your initial search does not generate many findings you may need to expand your search into other areas. Alternatively, you may need to narrow your search if you are initially faced with a vast number of potentially useful articles. Putting limits on the search or the focus of the search will make the search more manageable.

You may also be required to submit details of your search strategy as part of an academic assignment. It is a useful discipline to get in the habit of including in an appendix for any postgraduate assignments any literature searches undertaken as part of the assignment.

Searching other sources

Other sources of information that you may wish to search include the following.

- **Textbooks** – books can give you specific or general information and may be a good starting point. However, research published in books may well be dated as it takes quite a long time to publish and print a book after completion and some contemporary professional issues are changing constantly.
- **Government agencies and bodies,** such as the Department of Health.
- **Professional bodies,** such as Health Professions Council, Nursing and Midwifery Council or Health and Care Professions Council.
- **Patient/service user advocacy groups,** such as, for example, MIND.

You may also want to look for material that is not yet published in peer-reviewed journals. Literature that is not published or available through the usual bibliographic sources such as information databases is known as 'grey literature'. It is often information that has been conveyed by another route such as a conference presentation or a report. Grey literature may be useful to find cutting-edge information on a subject but you need to be aware that findings may not have been subject to critical scrutiny in the way that published material has. Coad (2006) provides a useful article on searching for and utilising grey literature (see Further reading at the end of this chapter).

3. Obtain copies of the appropriate literature generated by the search

It is likely that most of the references generated by your search will be found in journals. For articles available in full text electronically, you can either print them off or download them to your hard drive or a memory stick for future use. For journal articles not available as full text, you will need to check if your university library holds hard copies of the journal – usually held in bound volumes. Your librarian will also be able to assist you in locating journals not held locally, which may require a visit or contact with other libraries to arrange an inter-library loan. Obviously this may be quite time-consuming and there may be costs involved, so it is important to discriminate between key papers that are essential and those that may be of interest but not essential. This is known as selectivity. It is also crucial not to underestimate the time it takes not just to search for but also to actually obtain good quality information sources.

Reading and note-taking skills

Francis Bacon (1561–1626) is widely cited as having stated: 'some books are to be tasted, others to be swallowed, and some few to be chewed and digested' (Bacon, cited in Moncur, 2007). This selective approach also applies to the literature retrieved from a search. Papers and articles must be read to decide on those worthy of full analysis and those that can be rejected once you have scanned them for relevance. This is about 'getting to know' your literature.

A five-stage technique to develop reading skills was developed by Robinson (1970). The technique is known as SQ3R and is widely recommended as a useful tool for students in study skill texts.

1. **Survey** the document. Scan the abstract if available and have a quick look at the conclusions to get a brief overview of the text. Decide if it is likely to be of any help. If not, discard it.
2. **Question.** As you begin the process of reading, ensure you have developed some questions around the subject. The answers to these questions are almost the goals of your literature search, and may help you to structure the information in your own mind.
3. **Read.** Read through the document in detail, engaging in active reading. This means trying to work out the main ideas within the piece and perhaps considering how far this links with other reading you have done or, indeed, with your own experiences.
4. **Recall.** To assist in memorising, try to remember key findings without looking. Identify core facts or essential information within the article.
5. **Review.** Once you have recalled the information, you can move on to the stage of reviewing it. This review can be done by re-reading the document and by expanding your notes.

Note-taking should commence at stage 3 as you begin to read through your literature in depth. Using highlighter pens to highlight key aspects of papers and annotating on the paper itself may be useful strategies in making sense of literature. You cannot possibly remember all the key issues and questions generated from the papers and texts that you read, so clear legible notes will both support your ability to think critically around the topic and enable you to manage the literature reviewed and use it in future studies.

ACTIVITY

Consider how you currently manage the process of reading and note-taking following a literature search. Is there scope for improving the systems you use for note-taking and for retaining and accessing the notes at a later date?

Having effective reading and note-taking skills is particularly important in postgraduate study because of the vast amount of reading required as you gain mastery of your subject. A full review of note-taking strategies is provided in study skills texts such as Cottrell's book (Cottrell, 2008), but some key guidance on note-taking includes:

- keep notes brief – write in phrases and use abbreviations;
- use your own words;
- note key words and main ideas;
- use headings, number points and link up points using arrows and dotted lines;
- make sure full reference of article is given;
- write quotations in a different colour to stand out.

(Cottrell, 2008, p. 123)

Ensure that you organise your notes by using separate sheets of paper or small cards for each article. File them under different topic areas for ease of retrieval.

Shields (2009) makes an important point about 'note-making', in that it differs from 'note-taking'. He suggests that note-taking is something that you might do during a lecture, for example, and is a fairly passive activity in which you are copying or paraphrasing what the lecturer is saying. However, note-making is much more of a learning process and involves summarising, evaluating and considering the quality of the work.

The importance of meticulously recording the sources for your note-taking, and carefully differentiating between your own thoughts and ideas and those of others cannot be overemphasised if plagiarism is to be avoided.

Avoiding plagiarism

You will obviously be aware of the seriousness of plagiarism from your undergraduate studies. However, because it is increasingly recognised as a problem by universities and across the wider scientific community (Caldwell, 2008) it is worthy of revision. Plagiarism is unfair academic practice and has been defined as 'the substantial, unacknowledged incorporation into a student's work of material derived from the work (published or unpublished) of another' (Stinson, 2003, p.1). Attempting to pass off the work of others as your own, either consciously or through ignorance, is not only cheating (in terms of potentially getting academic recognition dishonestly) but is also a violation of trust and a threat to the integrity of the wider academic world. In addition, a literature review by Harper (2006) suggests a relationship between academic dishonesty and unethical professional behaviours in nurses. For this reason, plagiarism by students on professional courses may be treated even more seriously than by students undertaking non-vocational studies.

Yakovchuk (2004) suggests the problem of '... "patch writing", which involves altering an original text by substituting synonyms or changing grammatical structures, seems to be a common practice among both learner and expert writers'. In other words, plagiarism may not just involve copying the work of others, but also their ideas. Plagiarism may therefore include:

- paraphrasing the work of others, without acknowledging the source;
- presenting key ideas or concepts developed without acknowledging them as such;
- using the work of fellow students as your own;
- citing the work of your lecturers without attributing it as such.

However, it is relatively easy to avoid plagiarism by following certain rules. Cottrell (2008, p. 128) suggests that you:

- write all notes in your own words;
- note down exactly where you read the information you put in your notes;
- write out where ideas and information come from:
  - reference your work meticulously,
  - make it clear when you are using direct quotations,
  - write a full list of references.

Get into the habit of starting your reference list for any assignment early on – this will ensure you do not have to spend time finding out where you sourced a particular piece of information or quotation.

To assist in the detection of plagiarised work, a range of electronic software packages has been developed in recent years. These enable electronically submitted assignments to be scanned to assess originality. They are increasingly being used by universities as tools to enable students to check their own work prior to submissions.

ACTIVITY

Check if your university provides guidance on avoiding plagiarism, including the availability of electronic software packages, as part of the university virtual learning environment, and find out what the university or faculty policy is on the use of this software by students.

4. Critically appraise the evidence in the literature

Once you have a range of papers or texts, the next stage is to carefully review the quality of each article. This is known as the process of critical appraisal. An excellent summary of the rationale and process for critical appraisal is provided in a downloadable free eight-page guide by the Centre for Evidence Based Medicine (2009). The guide defines critical appraisal as 'the process of assessing and interpreting evidence by systematically considering its validity, results and relevance to an individual's work'.

Therefore, critical appraisal enables you to determine the paper's strengths or limitations and, crucially, to evaluate the contribution that each paper makes to answering your own research or information question or questions.

Prior to systematically undertaking an in-depth review of each paper, it is helpful to do a quick assessment of quality. The list below provides a fairly broad list of prompt questions that could assist with this.

- Who is the author and what is their professional background?
- When was it published? This in itself should not necessarily lead you to exclude a source of evidence. A piece of research or a paper produced by a leading expert some years previously may well have authority and currency if nothing new has been added to that particular body of knowledge since. This is known as a seminal paper.
- Is the depth, breadth and scope of the topic coverage appropriate for inclusion in your sources?
- Where is it published? Is it published in a peer-reviewed journal? Peer review is an essential component of scholarly activity. It is a mechanism to ensure that material, prior to publication, has been subject to the scrutiny of experts in the field. Individual academic journals will have a range of peer reviewers who scrutinise and assess the quality of submitted papers to assist the editor in any decision about fitness for publication. It is worth mentioning here a list of the reasons suggested by Greenhalgh (1997) why research papers may be rejected by academic journals – see Figure 4.

In addition, once the paper is published, peer review enables other experts in the field to engage in debate on the findings through subsequent articles and correspondence. In this way the process of peer review not only helps to assure the quality of published papers, but also adds to the body of knowledge in a particular discipline.

Having done a quick assessment of the quality of the articles using these prompts, you may decide at this stage to further exclude some texts or papers. You are now ready to start systematically evaluating each individual paper.

If we return to the definition of critical appraisal given at the start of this section, the importance of 'considering its validity' is mentioned. In this context, validity means how

- The study did not address an important scientific issue.
- The study was not original (someone else had already done the same or a similar study).
- The study did not actually test the authors' hypothesis.
- A different type of study should have been done.
- Practical difficulties (in recruiting subjects, for example) led the authors to compromise on the original study protocol.
- The sample size was too small.
- The study was uncontrolled or inadequately controlled.
- The statistical analysis was incorrect or inappropriate.
- The authors drew unjustified conclusions from their data.
- There is a significant conflict of interest.

Figure 4. *Why research papers may be rejected for publication (Greenhalgh, 1997)*

far the information is authentic, accurate and truthful. In a research paper, this may mean considering the degree to which the research method actually measures what it purports to measure. It also means considering how far any conclusions drawn by the author are logical and consistent with the evidence presented. Moran (2000) suggests that there are five areas where potential flaws or inconsistencies in arguments may be seen. These are:

- the claims may be made on inaccurate or inadequate information;
- the reasoning processes may be invalid;
- the arguments may be based on questionable assumptions;
- statements made may be misleading – this is when, regardless of the truth of the statement itself, the particular point has no bearing on the argument;
- the use of circular arguments, when the same statement is used for both the premise of the argument and also the conclusion.

(adapted from Moran, 2009, pp. 94–6)

Essentially the process of critical appraisal acknowledges that not all literature is equal in terms of its quality. It enables the author to discriminate between robust and weak sources of evidence. In 1979 the Canadian Task Force on the Periodic Health Examination developed a more formal approach to assessing the quality of health and bio-scientific research that is known as a hierarchy of evidence (Canadian Task Force on the Periodic Health Examination, 1979).

ACTIVITY

What do you understand by a hierarchy of evidence?

A hierarchy of evidence

This is a process for ranking health and related research according to its quality. Since 1979, hierarchies of evidence are often used in health care to demonstrate the effectiveness of a particular practice according to the evidence available, and they are particularly used in the development of clinical guidelines, including national guidance from the National Institute for Health and Clinical Excellence (NICE) (NICE, 2009). In essence, this hierarchical approach to ranking evidence recognises the greater strength of evidence generated by systematic reviews and multicentre studies because the findings have been derived from multiple populations, settings and circumstances. Thus, expert opinion is clearly ranked lower than research methodologies but clearly has more rigour and validity then anecdotal evidence.

A range of hierarchies are recognised in health and bioscience literature, but the ranking outlined in Figure 5 is typical.

Level	Description
One	Strong evidence from at least one systematic review of well-designed randomised controlled trials (RCTs) e.g. Meta-analyses
Two	Evidence from at least one properly designed RCT of appropriate size
Three	Evidence from well-designed trials without randomisation – cohort, time series, or matched case controlled studies
Four	Evidence from well-designed non-experimental studies from more than one centre or research group
Five	Opinions from respected authorities, based on clinical evidence, descriptive studies or reports from committees
Six	Views of colleagues / peers

Figure 5. *A hierarchy of evidence (source: EBNP, 2013)*

It is important to be aware that the concept of a hierarchy of evidence has been questioned and critiqued (McQueen, 2002; Petticrew and Roberts, 2003; O'Halloran *et al.*, 2010).

ACTIVITY

What criticisms can be levelled at the notion of a hierarchy of evidence?

Questions and criticism you might want to consider include the following: are different research methodologies appropriate for different research questions? Petticrew and Roberts (2003) make the point that a hierarchy of evidence that ranks randomised controlled trials (RCTs) above other forms of enquiry:

> … obscures the synergistic relation between RCTs and qualitative research, and (particularly in the case of social and public health interventions) the fact that both sorts of research are often required in tandem; robust evidence of outcomes comes from randomised controlled trials but evidence of the process by which those outcomes were achieved, the quality of implementation of the intervention, and the context in which it occurred is likely to come from qualitative and other data.

(Petticrew and Roberts, 2003, p. 528)

In other words, quantitative research methods such as RCTs are not necessarily superior to qualitative methods, but rather they both offer different perspectives on a problem. An in-depth analysis of the differences between the quantitative and qualitative research paradigm can be found in any good research text (see the recommended further reading at the end of this chapter) but it is important to note that to rely only on quantitative research methods may not enable full exploration of a problem to be carried out. In addition, in the health or social care setting, it may not be ethical to carry out a randomised controlled trial on a particular intervention, in which case a cohort study may be the best type of research.

Although the notion of an absolute hierarchy of research evidence can be criticised, hierarchies do provide a useful starting point for considering the quality of evidence. However, it is important to acknowledge that hierarchies of evidence are only useful if a range of research on a particular area is available. In the absence of any robust research, the best evidence available on a topic may well be expert consensus. What is important is that in searches for evidence, whether to inform academic work or to use in professional practice, the best available evidence is retrieved.

Critical appraisal tools

In order to facilitate the process of critical appraisal, a range of critical appraisal tools, in the form of pro-formas, are available to guide the evaluation of different types of research.

A particularly useful free resource is the internet website the Critical Appraisal Skills Programme (CASP) at **www.casp-uk.net**. This provides a range of individual appraisal tools on different research methods that can be downloaded for free, including appraisal tools for:

- systematic reviews;
- RCTs;
- qualitative research;
- economic evaluation studies;
- cohort studies;
- case-control studies;
- diagnostic test studies.

Guidance on critically appraising non-empirical sources of material – such as discussion articles, textbooks or web-based material – can be found in Aveyard's book (2009) on undertaking a literature review.

The importance of critical appraisal skills for health and social care professionals

Both government policy and professional self-regulatory bodies have advocated the importance of critical appraisal skills for health professionals over the past 15 years (Department of Health, 1996; Nursing and Midwifery Council, 2008). Indeed, in 1998 the NHS Executive produced an information resource for nurses, midwives and health visitors advocating the importance of being 'clinically effective' in professional practice, which included the ability to: '… search literature to find out exactly what makes up clinically effective practice' [and] '… appraise all available information critically to decide on its relevance to day to day care' (NHS Executive, 1998, p. 4).

ACTIVITY

List the reasons why critical appraisal skills are important for the health and social care professional.

Some of the reasons in your list might include:

- the importance of practice being based on the best evidence possible, which requires professionals to scrutinise practice and assess it against robust research evidence;
- to ensure health and social care professionals can facilitate empowered decision-making with patients or clients by presenting the most current evidence available in an objective way;
- appraisal skills link closely to concepts of lifelong learning and continued professional development in terms of the professional engaging in wide reading and being able to challenge, critique and engage in debate on published material in their specialty;

- critical appraisal skills support the development of the critical thinker – as demonstrated in Chapter 2, critical thinking among health and social care staff is associated with better decision-making, enabling the professional to cope more effectively with the complexities of real life practice.

The notion of best practice is clearly underpinned by the belief that health and social care professionals will make decisions based on evaluation of the empirical evidence related to what works best in a particular clinical or practice scenario. Critical appraisal skills are therefore crucial, not just for academic work but also for assuring quality in professional practice for health and social care students.

5. Apply the key findings to your work

Once you have evaluated and appraised the literature that you have obtained from your search, the final stage is to utilise the findings within your academic or professional work. This involves:

- identifying the key findings or themes within the literature;
- interpreting the findings – this means considering what the implications of the findings are for your particular area of study, but also if there are any wider implications like, for example, for health and social policy development;
- identifying any gaps in the literature and suggesting areas for possible further research or study.

Further guidance on integrating the findings into your written work will be provided in Chapter 5, which explores the key characteristics of effective writing at Master's level in detail.

SUMMARY

This chapter encourages postgraduate students to acknowledge the importance of being able to retrieve and critique evidence to inform both their academic studies and their professional practice. A systematic approach to recognising information needs, converting these into search terms, a search for high-quality texts and papers and the ability to evaluate them for relevance and rigour has been described. Organising and utilising information is a key skill of the postgraduate student and investing time to develop and refine these skills is crucial.

Critical reflection	
Identify at least three things that you have learned from this chapter.	1. 2. 3.
How do you plan to use this knowledge?	1. 2. 3.
How will you evaluate the effectiveness of your plan?	1. 2. 3.
What further knowledge and evidence do you need?	1. 2. 3.

FURTHER READING

Aveyard, H. (2009) *Doing a Literature Review in Health and Social Care: A Practical Guide.* Maidenhead: McGraw-Hill
This is a useful book taking the reader through the full process of searching and appraising literature, synthesising findings and presenting a literature review.

Neale, J. (Ed.) (2009) *Research Methods for Health and Social Care.* Basingstoke: Palgrave
This is a clearly written text providing a full overview of different research methodologies and includes two useful chapters of the literature review and the systematic review.

NHS Evidence **www.evidence.nhs.uk**
Funded by the Department of Health, this website provides free access to national and local clinical and non-clinical information for health and social care. The search engine enables users to access health research, guidelines and government policy. In addition, NHS staff who have an Athens account can also get free access to some full text journals via the site.

Coad, J. (2006) 'Searching for and using grey literature'. *Nursing Times*, 102 (50): 35–36
This useful article provides tips and links for obtaining non-published material such as conference papers.

5

WRITING AT MASTER'S LEVEL

This chapter covers the following key issues:

- academic writing as a postgraduate skill;
- key characteristics of Master's level writing;
- key writing genres/styles;
- planning and preparing for writing at Master's level;
- organising and structuring an essay;
- referencing skills.

By the end of this chapter you should be able to:

- discuss the expectations and processes of written work at Master's level;
- critically reflect upon your own writing skills and identify areas for development;
- discuss the processes involved in writing a coherent, well developed essay;
- reference your work correctly using the Harvard referencing system.

INTRODUCTION

Academic writing, in its broadest sense, can be defined as 'writing that fulfils a purpose of education in a college or university' (Thaiss and Zawacki, 2006). Writing at Master's level has been described as a specialist activity (Atherton, 2005; Craswell, 2005) in the sense that postgraduate course requirements dictate purpose and remit at a specific level. In order to study at Master's level, there will, generally, be an expectation that students will have successfully demonstrated the ability to write academically (Atherton, 2005).

Assessment requirements at Master's level predominantly involve some form of writing. The QAA (2010) identifies a number of assessment methods, any of which may be utilised to assess your developing postgraduate knowledge and skills. These include:

- essays;
- practical reports or portfolios;
- dissertations or other output from research/project work;
- written examinations;
- problem-solving exercises;
- oral presentations;
- posters;
- placement reports.

It is clear that most of these involve writing and, as such, you will need to further develop your writing skills at Master's level if you are to demonstrate your in-depth knowledge effectively (through your writing) and successfully achieve your Master's degree.

ACTIVITY

What do you think the purposes of assignments are?

Giles and Hedge (2002, cited in Gatrell, 2006) clarify this by suggesting that the purposes of assignments are:

- to reinforce and consolidate learning;
- to evaluate learning;
- to demonstrate knowledge and understanding;
- to apply theoretical concepts to the real world.

It could be suggested that it is mainly through writing that postgraduate students demonstrate the characteristics of Master's graduates (QAA, 2010), as discussed in Chapter 1.

Submitting written work to the scrutiny of others can feel daunting and perhaps a little threatening, and this is understandable. Even the most experienced writers have concerns that their work will not be of an acceptable standard and, as such, will be negatively criticised.

This chapter will explore and discuss the requirements and expectations of written work at Master's level. It will allow you to consider, evaluate and further develop your academic writing skills and writing style to increase your confidence and competence. The chapter should be read in conjunction with Chapter 2 on critical thinking, Chapter 3 on becoming an independent learner and Chapter 4 on finding and using literature.

EXPECTATIONS OF WRITTEN WORK AT MASTER'S LEVEL

Atherton (2005) has suggested that, at postgraduate level, there is an expectation that you will have mastered the basic 'rules' of academic writing and states:

> ... I believe it is reasonable to expect that anyone who goes around with the letters MA after their name – which places them in some kind of intellectual elite – has an obligation to be able to express themselves clearly and literately.

ACTIVITY

What do you consider are the basic rules of expressing yourself clearly and literately?

Atherton identifies the following.

- Writing is intelligently structured using appropriate models or frameworks like, for example, models of guided reflection if writing a reflective piece.
- Paragraphs are correctly used – one key issue/idea per paragraph. In this way you construct a clear argument or make a clear case for your discussion.
- Style is clear and professional, with no abbreviations or slang.
- Sentence construction, grammar and syntax are correct.
- An absolute understanding of what plagiarism means (see Chapter 4).
- References are presented correctly in the text and in the reference list.

In addition to work being literate, there will be other criteria for Master's level writing. Craswell (2005, p. xv) identifies these as follows:

> Conciseness in writing is valued in general by the academic community, as is treating information critically, attending to audience needs, consistency in the mechanics of academic writing, careful referencing of sources, coherent development of texts, sound logic and evidential support in arguments.

Atherton (2005) largely concurs with Craswell (2005) while also offering some further useful criteria for work at Master's level.

1. It addresses the module outcomes.
2. It has evidence.
3. It is critical.
4. It explores implicit values – '... it is easy to write about what should or ought or must happen. But at M level you are expected to dig behind these self-evident truths and to expose the assumptions behind them and to entertain the potential alternatives'.
5. It contextualises.

6. It pursues an argument.

7. It does not try to say everything about nothing – an assignment topic needs to be tightly defined.

8. It brings something of you into it – '… you are drawing on all the knowledge and experience you have accumulated thus far, and doing something with it …'.

You need to consider Atherton's last point carefully – that postgraduate writing should bring something of you into it.

ACTIVITY

What does 'bringing something of you into it' mean?

You may have considered that you need to demonstrate the ability to synthesise the issues relevant to your subject with your own professional experience. This is wider than just providing examples to illustrate understanding of theory. It means applying appropriate theory, concepts and paradigms to systematically investigate issues relating to your own professional work. An awareness of how the skills you have developed through your postgraduate study inform your professional practice is crucial in your work.

In summary, writing is a key skill that will need to be further developed to enable you to effectively develop your arguments and demonstrate your postgraduate knowledge and skills. Indeed, the absolute foundation of postgraduate academic writing is critical analysis. This is what differentiates writing at postgraduate level from that of undergraduate writing. Postgraduate writing goes beyond description and discussion that simply accepts information as it is. Writing at this higher level involves evaluating information before accepting or rejecting it, while also providing appropriate evidence for doing so.

TYPES OF ACADEMIC WRITING

Generally, assessment at postgraduate level will involve producing work from different academic genres.

ACTIVITY

What is meant by 'different academic genres'?

You will need to become familiar with those academic genres relevant for your studies in order to successfully progress through your course. Some may be unfamiliar and you will therefore need to understand, for example, the specific style, language and structure of each. You will also need to understand the specific writing practices and conventions that are associated with the discipline being studied and the institution where you are studying.

ACTIVITY

Spend some time familiarising yourself with the expectations of your specific course, with particular focus on the assessment requirements and the academic genres.

There are many different genres or types of academic writing including lecture notes, analytical essays, research proposals, scientific reports, reflective essays, dissertations, journal articles and books. Each type or genre has a different purpose and a different language depending on audience. For example, a research proposal will be written in a different style to a research report or dissertation, with the different purpose requiring a different process. Each of these will be written in the third person, as contrasted with a reflective essay that may well be written in the first person. Specific differences between essays, reports and reflective pieces will be considered in detail towards the end of the chapter but it is important to acknowledge here that different institutions set out the criteria for each of the assignments you will be required to produce and, again, it is important to familiarise yourself with the specific requirements before you commence writing.

Writing and presenting essays

An essay is a short piece of prose that is produced to a specific set of writing conventions (Cottrell, 2003). It is generally written in a formal, academic style and needs to be grammatically sound. Essays are one of the most common forms of assessment within higher education and there will be some expectation at Master's level that you have understood and successfully demonstrated some basic techniques prior to commencing your course. If you feel that your essay-writing skills require major development, or that essay writing is a major part of your course, then you may find it useful to read books with a specific focus on developing academic writing skills. Further resources relating to this are identified at the end of this chapter. Leeds Metropolitan University (2009) identifies conventions relating to essay writing as follows.

- Writing should be in continuous text, although sometimes an essay might have sections with subheadings. Paragraphs should be effectively used to break the text up into readable chunks. The onus is always on the essay writer to organise his or her writing in such a way that it is easy for the reader to follow.
- The essay is formal in both structure and language. It should have a well-defined introduction, body, and conclusion. Standard English should be used as opposed to colloquial English.
- Essays can vary in length anywhere from 500 to 5000 words. Such a range is not set in stone, but shorter pieces might constitute some form of brief reflection, whereas longer pieces of writing would probably be called projects, theses or dissertations.

- The English word 'essay' is derived from the French *essai*, meaning 'a try'. It is worth bearing the original meaning in mind. Historically, the essay has been a means of expressing everyday concerns or reflections and not a format used to express ultimate answers to things. The modern university essay differs considerably from its historical cousin, yet something of its older ethos remains. As a student writer, you will not be expected to produce an ultimate answer, but rather to 'try' your best to produce a plausible answer to a topic that probably has no set or singular answer.

Additionally, you will also need to adhere to set conventions relating to the presentation of your work. You may find specific information regarding your own institution's presentation requirements in your course or module handbooks.

ACTIVITY

What do you think are important aspects with regard to the presentation of work? Write a list of your key points.

You may have considered some or all of the following.

- Identification of your work on the front page – for example, student number, course, title of assignment.
- Word-processing of work with no typographical errors.
- Spacing and margins.
- Logical organisation of work with clearly defined paragraphs, headings (if appropriate) and inclusion of word count.
- Work presented in an appropriate form – for example, a folder, binder, etc.

As already mentioned, you will need to check the specific requirements for your course.

Essay planning

Before you start writing your paper or essay, your lecturer should have had some initial discussions with you, either as part of a large group or on an individual basis as part of a tutorial. You do need to have a good understanding of what is expected of you before you start. If the assignment remit is unclear to you, you run the risk of not answering the assignment brief correctly and therefore there is the possibility of failure. Writing an excellent answer to an unset question will result in a penalty and possibly a fail and you will be penalised similarly if you stray too far from the set word limit. Therefore, to minimise this risk, you should ensure that you fully understand the assignment criteria including any word limit and presentation requirements. If you are at all unsure, you should arrange to discuss this with your lecturer.

ACTIVITY

Reflect on a time when you were asked to complete an academic assignment or task. How did you organise yourself and the work itself to ensure it was completed effectively?

Cottrell (2003) identifies a seven-point plan that will assist the development and writing of your essay (see Figure 1). Dividing the task into various activities will give some structure that may support you with your time management and also make the task feel less daunting.

1. Clarify the task – make sure you know what you are looking for.
2. Collect and record information – get the information you need but be focused.
3. Organise and plan – organise your work as you go along.
4. Reflect and evaluate – when you have gathered the information think about where you have got to e.g. what have you discovered, has your viewpoint changed?
5. Write an outline plan and first draft – structure your writing.
6. Work on your first draft – develop and improve your writing.
7. Final drafts – edit, check and refine your final draft.

Figure 1. *A seven-point procedure for writing essays (Cottrell, 2003, p.152)*

Additionally, at Master's level there is a requirement that you demonstrate the ability to critically analyse theoretical concepts and ideas. With this in mind, it is important that you consider carefully your own ideas and how you will develop these as your work progresses. Therefore you do need to consider in some depth:

- the implications of the title;
- the ideas relating to the title;
- what it is that you are specifically being asked to explore;
- what kinds of examples from your practice you can use to strengthen your discussions.

Do not worry if things feel more complicated and complex at this stage. This is normal and somewhat inevitable as you consider various ideas and concepts and attempt to make sense of them. You will be expected to find your own perspective and apply theoretical concepts to your own professional practice. You will need to examine the literature (see Chapter 4) in some depth as you critically evaluate your findings in terms of rigour and relevance.

Structuring and organising an essay

The four key parts to an essay are:

- introduction;
- main body;
- conclusion;
- references.

ACTIVITY

What do you need to consider including within the four key parts of an essay?

The introduction

> Your approach to the question, your understanding of the question and the content you intend to cover.

(University of Worcester, 2010, p. 46)

The introduction should be utilised as a signpost for the reader regarding what you intend to cover within the essay and how you intend to do this. Therefore a detailed discussion of your aims and objectives is required. Your aims should demonstrate what you hope the assignment will clarify and/or critique in tackling the topic or title of the assignment. Including some of the key essay title words within the introduction will facilitate focus. You may also wish to include a statement relating to the value and relevance of this assignment to health and social care practice generally, or your specific professional area of practice.

You also need to include a statement of the scope of your assignment. It is unrealistic to think that you will be able to cover all aspects of a particular subject or issue within the word limit so you will need to give this careful consideration. Identify what you have chosen to focus upon and why, but also what you are not focusing upon and why. This will demonstrate that, through your reading, you have developed an awareness of other issues surrounding the topic but that you acknowledge that you do not have the space to consider all issues in depth.

It is useful to summarise how you intend to sequence your discussions at the end of the introduction. This aids readability and acts as an advance organiser for the reader. A clear introduction always improves the organisational style of a piece of work and may facilitate focus for you as the writer.

The body of the assignment

> Each paragraph should contain a theme or topic, backed up by supporting arguments and analysis. You should include other writers' ideas and arguments ... You need to analyse the material and give your views.
>
> (University of Worcester, 2010, p. 47)

This section is the heart of the essay and is your opportunity to demonstrate your in-depth knowledge and understanding within your specific area of study (QAA, 2010). It is clear that you will not be able to include all issues relating to a particular topic so you will need to be selective and identify the most important issues for consideration. By doing this you will be able to consider and critically analyse issues in the depth required at postgraduate level.

Assessment criteria at Master's level will include some aspect of critical analysis. This means you must move beyond description. You must examine and weigh up the evidence and determine your own perspective, using the literature to support your discussions (see Chapters 2 and 4). You will also be expected to write concisely and get points across as clearly and precisely as possible.

Through identifying, discussing and utilising appropriate theories you should be able to demonstrate your understanding of the issues and also demonstrate skills in evaluation and, as previously mentioned, critique. Utilising these skills effectively will enable you to usefully comment on and contextualise issues while adding your own views to the debate. This is expected at Master's level, as indeed is evidence of initiative and independent thought (QAA, 2010).

The conclusion

> A summary of the essay showing the conclusions of your analysis of the evidence presented.
>
> (University of Worcester, 2010, p. 47)

The final section of your assignment is the conclusion. It is useful to begin with a summary of the key findings or arguments, considering only the most significant outcomes. The conclusion should not raise any issues or new material that has not previously been identified or discussed. You should relate the content to the literature that has been reviewed and take a stance – did you reach the same conclusions or not and, if not, why not? This may relate to consideration of the issues from a different professional viewpoint and/or context.

You should utilise the conclusion to further enhance overall cohesion by referring back to the introduction and your aims. You should identify whether you have met your aims or not and, again, explain why this might be. You should identify any weaknesses or limitations that may have constrained your discussions and conclusions. These are inevitable – acknowledging them does not suggest weakness but rather strengthens the work as it demonstrates critical thinking skills.

Finally, your conclusion should clearly indicate any implications or recommendations for practice that you can make based on your previous discussions. A useful way to end the conclusion is to identify any future areas of research that may have been identified through your discussions. As has been discussed previously, Master's level study frequently raises many new questions as well as answering the ones you initially wished to explore. This is a key point and is expected at this higher level.

Referencing

There is an expectation at postgraduate level that students will read widely and acknowledge their sources throughout their work. You will therefore need to ensure you have an understanding of how to accurately acknowledge and reference source materials, both within the text and the reference list.

Your sources are important in terms of the arguments and position you adopt within your written work and, as such, they must be acknowledged. Failure to conform to an agreed referencing style may be construed as plagiarism (see Chapter 4).

The two most common referencing styles utilised within academia are the 'author–date' style and the 'numerical' style.

- Author–date style
  - References are acknowledged within the text and there is an alphabetical list of references (by author name) in a list at the end of the work. This style includes the Harvard referencing system.

- Numbered style
  - There is a numerical list of references that is organised according to the order in which the works appear in the text. This style includes the Vancouver system.

You do need to be aware of the specific referencing requirements for your course and these may be included within your course handbook.

ACTIVITY

Find out which referencing style is utilised at your institution and on your course. Identify a referencing guide and other referencing resources that will support your studies.

Higher education institutions generally provide details of their preferred system and these will usually be available in a published form at the library and/or via an online learning resource. The Harvard system is widely adopted within higher education (Denby *et al.*, 2008).

ACTIVITY

Undertake the following quiz to assess your referencing skills. Identify areas where you may need to improve.

Harvard Referencing Quiz

1. **Using Harvard referencing, suggest two ways in which this quotation could be cited in your text. It comes from research undertaken by John Haimes in 2004.**

   pain and anxiety are inextricably linked

2. **How could the above quotation be paraphrased in your text?**

3. **Correct the following references:**
   - (Shelley and Jones, 1999) stated that in order to use reflection as a learning tool it is essential to use a structured framework.
   - Brown hypothesised that an increase in the ratio of trained to untrained staff may not necessarily have a positive impact on care.
   - Other studies have been found to agree with these findings (Black, Smith, Bloggs and Casey, 2001; Akram 1999).

4. **Which is generally considered the correct citation in the following reference list, using the Harvard system?**
   - Jones DW, 2000. 'The oranginess of oranges' in *Fresh Fruit Monthly*.
   - 1) Jones, D.W. (2000) The oranginess of oranges. *Fresh Fruit Monthly*. 14,6, 78–84
   - DW Jones. The oranginess of oranges. *Fresh Fruit Monthly*. No.14 pages 78 to 84, year 2000
   - Jones, D.W. (2000) 'The oranginess of oranges'. *Fresh Fruit Monthly* 14,6,78–84

5. **You are using Harvard style and you need to reference two papers published by the same author in the same year. For example:**

   Jones 2000, 'The oranginess of oranges' and Jones 2000 'The fruit I like'.

   How are they displayed in the reference list? Choose one of the following,
   - Define them by month of publication, e.g. Jones (June 2000) and Jones (August 2000).
   - Define the first as Jones (1, 2000) and the second as Jones (2, 2000).

- Define the first as Jones (2000a) and the second as Jones (2000b).
- Just reference as normal, the titles of the citations should be enough to decide which is which.

6. **You have made reference to a book. What is normal to include in the reference list?**
   - Publisher's name.
   - Publisher's name and edition number.
   - Publisher's name, edition number and place of publication.
   - Publisher's name, edition number, place of publication and ISBN number.

7. **How would you cite a website in the reference list?**
   - Stokes, C.W. (2001) The iCT Project Website **www.shef.ac.uk/uni/projects/ictp/ archive.htm** The University of Sheffield [last accessed 24/05/01].
   - Stokes. C.W. (2001) **www.shef.ac.uk/uni/projects/ictp/archive.htm** [Accessed 24/05/01]
   - Stokes. C.W. (2001) The iCT Project Website Archive, The University of Sheffield.
   - The iCT Project Website (www.shef.ac.uk/uni/projects/ictp/archive.htm)

8. **What is wrong with these references in the reference list?**
   - Rowe J.A. Accountability: a fundamental component of an allied health professional's work British Journal of Dietetics 2000 9, 70, 334-339
   - Department of Health The NHS Plan NHS
   - Dimond B. Legal Aspects of nursing Prentice Hall 2000

Answers – Harvard Referencing Quiz

1. 'Pain and anxiety are inextricably linked' (Haimes, 2004, p. 6) Haimes (2004, p. 6) has stated: 'Pain and anxiety are inextricably linked'.

2. Haimes (2004) found a link between pain and anxiety in his research into …

3.
   - Shelley and Jones (1999) stated that …
   - Brown (2002) hypothesised that …
   - (Akram, 1999; Black *et al.*, 2001)

4. Jones, D.W. (2000) 'The oranginess of oranges'. *Fresh Fruit Monthly* 14,6,78–84

5. Define the first as Jones (2000a) and the second as Jones (2000b).

6. Publisher's name, edition number and place of publication.

7. Stokes, C.W. (2001) The iCT Project Website **www.shef.ac.uk/uni/projects/ictp/ archive.htm** The University of Sheffield [last accessed 24/05/01].

8.

- Rowe, J.A. (2000) 'Accountability: a fundamental component'. *British Journal of Dietetics* 9, 70, 334–339
- DH (2001) *The NHS Plan*. London: DH
- Dimond, B. (2001) *Legal aspects of nursing*. London: Prentice Hall

Acknowledging your sources and referencing correctly and consistently within the text and the reference list will enhance your work. It is important that there are no discrepancies between the references you have cited within the text and those included within the reference list. Referencing skills are relatively easy to learn and further develop. You should ensure you adhere to the recommended referencing style for your course and consult and follow the guidance you are given. Examples of how to reference in different circumstances are readily available. Indeed, you will see many examples within the literature as you progress your reading. Referencing can account for up to 10 per cent of the total marks available, therefore accurate referencing will ensure you do not lose any marks unnecessarily. Adopting a managed approach by keeping an ongoing, up-to-date record of your sources will facilitate success with your written work.

Assignment checklist

The following checklist should be used following completion of the first draft of your essay. This will facilitate further development of your work and allow you to focus on the key areas.

Introduction

- Is there a clear rationale for the topic area?
- Is there reference to the question being asked?
- Are the aims and objectives clear?
- Is there evidence of signposting with a clear summary of how discussions and ideas will be sequenced and developed?

The body

- Have key areas been included as outlined within the introduction?
- Does each paragraph have a clear focus and topic area?
- Is the literature appropriate and relevant for discussions?
- Is there sufficient evidence to support discussions/arguments?
- Does the work flow smoothly from one paragraph to another?
- Is literature effectively utilised within the essay and well incorporated within discussions?
- Are all references correctly cited in the text and the reference list?

Conclusion

- Is there an effective conclusion?
- Does the conclusion refer back to ideas stated in the introduction?
- Does the conclusion summarise the key findings?
- Does the conclusion offer appropriate suggestions based on the findings/issues?

Report writing

As a professional it is likely that you have some experience of writing reports as part of your professional practice.

ACTIVITY

Reflect on any previous activity in relation to report writing. What skills and knowledge did you require to undertake the task? Can you identify any developmental needs in relation to producing a report for academic assessment purposes?

As you may have realised, report writing is a skill that is valued in many disciplines (Race, 2007) and, as such, it is a useful assessment method within professionally focused courses. Reports are distinctive documents with a particular style that is quite different from that of essays. Gimenez (2007, p. 110) defines reports as documents that:

- have a very clear objective and a specific purpose;
- are written for a specific audience;
- have a distinctive structure and layout;
- contain information as well as recommendations.

As Gimenez (2007) identifies, reports have a specific convention with a specific structure and style that distinguishes them from essays. Cottrell (2003, p. 209) provides a useful comparison between reports and essay writing (see Figure 2).

Reports	Essays
Reports originate from outside an educational context: they are typical of writing required for the world of work.	Essays originate in academic settings: they are rarely used anywhere else.
Reports present research data and findings that you have collected yourself – through a laboratory experiment, a survey, a questionnaire or a case study, or by applying theory to your work placement or some other situation.	Essays focus on analysing or evaluating theory, past research by other people and ideas. They seldom present findings of new research.

Essays and reports have different structures:	
A report is divided into separate sections.	Essays do not have sections; they flow as a continuous piece of writing.
A report contains tables, charts and appendices.	Essays generally do not include tables or appendices.
Each section of the report is given a heading. Each point is numbered.	Essays do not include section headings or numbering.
Reports contain a mixture of writing styles, depending on the section.	Essays use a consistent writing style throughout.
Reports include descriptions of the methods used.	Essays should not refer to the method used in arriving at conclusions.
The description in a report should include brief comment on how the research could have been improved, and what gaps remain for further research.	Essays (analytical) generally do not do this. Essays are not usually reflective about the process of researching and writing the essay itself.
Reports often include recommendations for action.	Essays generally do not include recommendations.

Figure 2. *A comparison of reports and essays (adapted from Cottrell, 2003, p. 209)*

However, there are also some commonalities between essay writing and report writing in that the writing must be grammatically accurate, points should be made concisely and the style should be fluent. Report writing conventions can vary so it is important that you explore and understand the specific requirements for your course.

Reflective writing

Reflective writing differs from essay writing or report writing as the subject matter may result from personal experience and, as such, may be quite subjective, using the first person. Reflective writing for assessment purposes is utilised quite frequently within professionally focused courses in health and social care.

ACTIVITY

What is your understanding of reflection within professional practice?

The concept of reflection is defined by Moon (2004, p. 82) as:

> … a form of mental processing – like a form of thinking – that we may use to fulfil a purpose or to achieve some anticipated outcome or we may simply 'be reflective' and then an outcome can be unexpected. Reflection is applied to relatively complicated, ill structured ideas for which there is not an obvious solution and is largely based on the further processing of knowledge and understanding that we already possess.

The idea that reflection enables practitioners to gain further insight and understanding of complex practice situations, and indeed their own practice, has been viewed positively by health professional bodies and educationalists. This has resulted in reflection and reflective practice being widely incorporated into many professional courses (Moon, 2004).

Reflective practice is a relatively recent concept that came to be used in practice settings following the work of Schön (1983). The term 'reflective practice' encompasses the use of reflection within a professional context allowing practitioners to consider the complexities and unpredictability of practice situations in order to cope more effectively in the future (Moon, 2004). At Master's level, critical reflection on practice facilitates students to consider practice issues in greater depth and provides an opportunity to bring, as previously discussed in this chapter, 'something of you into it … you are drawing on all the knowledge and experience you have accumulated thus far, and doing something with it …' (Atherton, 2010).

Utilising a reflective framework

Utilising a reflective framework or model within your writing will enable you to consider and view experiences from different perspectives (Ashby, 2006).

ACTIVITY

Have you utilised reflective frameworks/models previously? Consider why you chose a particular framework and reflect on its effectiveness in achieving your aim.

Various frameworks are available, including Gibbs (1988) and Johns (1995), but you should choose a reflective framework that best suits your purpose. For example, if your focus is on an ethical issue you should choose a framework that best supports your thinking in this area. Johns' model identifies ethical knowing within the framework, drawing on Carper's work (1978), so utilising this model would enable you to focus on this area in greater depth. Using a framework, providing a rationale for its use and critically evaluating its use from a personal and practice perspective will give an added dimension to your work.

Reflection at Master's level

Moon (2004) identifies 'levels of reflection' as reflective activities, including reflective writing, that are a progression from description to much deeper forms of reflection. This 'depth' of reflection implies the higher thinking level that is a characteristic of Master's level study and, therefore, you should consider this in relation to the development of your reflective writing. Moon (2004, p.102) characterises depth of reflection as 'increased flexibility and ability to manage the framing process in an open and flexible manner'. She clarifies this further through a generic, developmental framework for reflective writing where reflective writing at its deepest level is identified as follows (see Figure 3).

- Description now only serves the process of reflection, covering the issues for reflection and noting their context. There is clear evidence of standing back from an event and there is mulling over and internal dialogue.

- The account shows deep reflection, and it incorporates a recognition that the frame of reference with which an event is viewed can change.

- A metacognitive stance is taken (i.e. critical awareness of one's own processes of mental functioning – including reflection).

- The account probably recognises that events exist in a historical or social context that may be influential on a person's reaction to them. In other words, multiple perspectives are noted.

- Self-questioning is evident (an 'internal dialogue' is set up at times) deliberating between different views of personal behaviour and that of others.

- The view and motives of others are taken into account and considered against those of the writer.

- There is recognition that prior experience and thoughts (one's own and others') can interact with the production of current behaviour.

- There is recognition of the role of emotion in shaping ideas and recognition of the manner in which different emotional influences can frame the account in different ways.

- There is observation that there is learning to be gained from the experience and points for learning are noted.

- There is recognition that the personal frame of reference can change according to the emotional state in which it is written, the acquisition of new information, the review of ideas and the effect of time passing.

Figure 3. *A generic framework for reflective writing (Moon, 2004, p. 214)*

This framework should support your reflective writing and enable you to consider clearly any developmental activities that you need to undertake to progress your reflective writing skills at Master's level.

SUMMARY

This chapter has encouraged postgraduate students to acknowledge the importance of being able to write effectively in order to successfully present academic arguments and an academic stance. A number of key writing genres/styles have been considered in relation to Master's level assessment and students have been presented with various tools, techniques and further resources to support their writing. Academic writing is a vehicle for students to demonstrate their developing knowledge, skills and understanding. Effective academic writing is a key requirement of postgraduate study and investing time to develop and refine these skills is crucial to ensuring success.

Critical reflection	
Identify at least three things that you have learned from this chapter.	1. 2. 3.
How do you plan to use this knowledge?	1. 2. 3.
How will you evaluate the effectiveness of your plan?	1. 2. 3.
What further knowledge and evidence do you need?	1. 2. 3.

FURTHER READING

Cottrell, S. (2008) *The Study Skills Handbook*. London: Palgrave.
This book is an excellent general study skills guide for all undergraduate or postgraduate students.

Another useful study skills guide is:
Lloyd, M. and Murphy, P. (2008) *Essential Study Skills for Health and Social Care*. Exeter: Reflect Press

Craswell, G. (2005) *Writing for Academic Success: A Postgraduate Guide*. London: Sage
This book provides a detailed guide to writing at postgraduate level with some useful exercises and examples.

Moon, J.A. (2004) *A Handbook of Reflective and Experiential Learning: Theory and Practice*. London: Routledge Falmer
This book provides some good, detailed discussion and analysis relating to reflection and there is a very useful resource section.

University of Worcester (2010) *Moving On: Academic Writing*. Available at: **www.worc. ac.uk/movingon/Academic%20writing.pdf** (last accessed 10 January 2013)
This guide provides a useful 'step-by-step' guide to academic writing and may be useful as a revision guide for students who have not studied for some time.

6

HOW TO GET PUBLISHED

This chapter covers the following key issues:

- the professional and personal benefits of publishing work;
- barriers to publication;
- the process of writing an article, from planning to responding to reviewers' comments;
- the ethical issues to consider when publishing;
- other types of scholarly activity the postgraduate student may wish to consider.

By the end of this chapter you should be able to:

- discuss the potential personal and professional benefits of getting your work published;
- review your own academic and professional work and its potential for publication;
- describe the factors to consider when choosing a journal for submission;
- demonstrate an awareness of the ethical issues to address in publishing;
- consider other types of scholarly activity that you could engage in to promote and disseminate your work.

INTRODUCTION

During any period of postgraduate study, students are likely to produce a range of written assignments ranging from reflective narratives to original research projects. Submitted work may have been undertaken with the support and supervision from academic staff and, once marked, the work will be complemented with the marker's comments and feedback. The potential for using work undertaken as part of a Master's programme to produce robust and informed articles of interest to others is therefore high. This chapter is focused on supporting Master's level students to get their work out to a wider audience through publication and other scholarly activity.

ACTIVITY

Why do you think it is important for professionals working in health and social care to publish and disseminate their work?

Keen (2007) has suggested that publishing by registered nurses is important because '... the development of nursing from a ritually based vocation to an emerging profession has created a need for a body of knowledge. This body is a hungry beast' (Keen, 2007, p. 383). This could equally apply to other professional groups in health and social care. Indeed, a paper by Staudt *et al.* (2003) suggested that social workers have an ethical responsibility to contribute to the knowledge base of social work and to contribute to the professional literature. This is because publishing your work supports the development of evidence-based practice by challenging health and social care practitioners to review and benchmark their own practice against the best. This should ultimately lead to improvements in the quality of care and treatment, demonstrated through better outcomes for patients or clients.

Students who undertake original research may be under an even stronger obligation to ensure the findings of their work are publicised. The Research Councils UK in its position statement (2006) on research outputs has stated that a key principle underpinning research is: 'Ideas and knowledge derived from publicly-funded research must be made available and accessible for public use, interrogation and scrutiny, as widely, rapidly and effectively as practicable' (Research Councils UK, 2006). A failure to disseminate the findings of research means that others researching into that field cannot take that work into account when planning future research projects and, in particular, the research could be repeated unnecessarily, with the associated waste of scarce resources. Failure to publish research is therefore, potentially, very significant. However, reluctance by nurses, midwives and social workers to publish research that they have undertaken is widely reported (Driscoll and Driscoll, 2002; Hicks, 1993; Staudt *et al.*, 2003). Reasons for this reluctance may include that, having spent so much time and effort in completing a thesis, the student no longer has the enthusiasm for returning to the project to do further work to summarise key aspects of the work into a short publishable article. One way of overcoming this may be to approach the academic who provided supervision for the work, who may well be very happy to work with the student to assist in the process of explicating, summarising and drafting an article. We will return to this in the section on collaborative writing.

For health and social care staff working in academic posts in UK universities, an additional pressure to publish any research that they have undertaken comes from the Research Excellence Framework (REF). The REF is an annual peer review exercise to evaluate the quality of research in UK higher-education institutions (Higher Education Funding Council, 2010). The audit focuses on published research and the assessment results inform the selective distribution of funds by the UK Higher Education Funding Council. So it is also crucial that academics publish the results of their research in order to improve both the financial and academic standing of the university.

As well as the wider benefits to the professions from publishing, there are obviously personal benefits for the individual that can be gained through the publishing process.

ACTIVITY

What are the potential personal benefits to individuals who have work published?

Some of the personal benefits you have listed might include:

- a sense of pride and achievement;
- the chance to develop writing and information management skills;
- the opportunity to receive feedback from editors, reviewers and readers;
- something impressive to add to your curriculum vitae, which may help career development;
- recognition of your expertise in a field – this in turn can lead to you being invited to engage in further scholarly activity in the specialty such as presenting at conferences, writing further papers or perhaps becoming a reviewer for a journal or publisher;
- financial benefits – a few journals pay a small fee on publication (although a word of caution – the fee is unlikely to reflect the actual time and effort that the novice writer exerts in producing a finished article).

ACTIVITY

List some of the reasons why health and social care professionals may be reluctant to develop and submit papers for publication.

Compare your own list of reasons for being reluctant to write for publication with the list suggested by Pugsley (2009) in Figure 1.

- I don't have enough time to write.
- I have too many good ideas.
- I find it hard to structure an article.
- I suffer from writer's block.
- I spend too much time rewriting.
- I am not sure when to write the title and the abstract.
- Other people keep correcting what I write.
- I don't know which journal to send my paper.
- Getting past the reviewers is a major problem.
- I don't know if I have written a good article.

Figure 1. *Reasons for not writing (Pugsley, 2009)*

You, like Pugsley, might have suggested that one of the biggest barriers to getting published is lack of time – and certainly this should not be underestimated. However, Boice and Jones (1984, cited in Steinert *et al.*, 2008) found in their research that highly productive authors had no more free time than less productive ones, which suggests that other factors may be more important in contributing to reluctance to engage in the process of publishing. These factors may include a lack of confidence or little belief in one's own abilities – Driscoll and Driscoll (2002) identify this as a challenge to aspiring writers. However, for postgraduate students this should be less of an issue. The formative and summative feedback you have received during your postgraduate studies should reassure you about your writing ability and the quality of your ideas and arguments.

Pugsley (2009) also makes the point that most writers are not naturally gifted and that '… writing is not a gift, it is a craft skill which needs to be worked at'. Indeed Hartley (2008) reviewed the research on successful writers and found a relationship between certain key criteria and productive writers. These writers:

- had regular work habits;
- were highly motivated;
- collaborated more than unproductive writers;
- were persistent in that they revised and resubmitted rejected papers;
- seized opportunities.

(Hartley, 2008, p. 177)

ACTIVITY

Self-assess yourself against the criteria associated with being a productive writer. How far do you think these are achievable for you?

If you self-assess yourself against these criteria, you can see that they are all learnt habits – if you are determined and prepared to put in the work there is no reason why you should not be successful.

WHAT SHOULD I WRITE ABOUT?

The first step is to consider what you are going to write about.

ACTIVITY

Consider work you have been involved in – either in your academic life as a student or in your professional practice – that might be of interest to others. Make a list of possible topics.

Starting with work you have already done

Academic work that you have produced might include literature reviews, original research, academic essays or conference presentations. Selecting from previous work is often a good starting point for the novice writer as you have already started the process of committing it to paper. However, it is likely that your work will require substantial development and rewriting to make it accessible to a different audience. Indeed, journal editors may well request different formats and word counts from those of your original targeted reader who was, for example, a university lecturer. It may be that you could develop several different articles from one piece of work – for example, if you decide to write up some original research that you have been involved in you will need to decide what aspect you are going to write about. A research dissertation, for example, may provide the scope for producing several different articles. Possibilities include:

- a report providing a summary and overview of the result;
- a summary of the literature review;
- a discussion of the particular research methodology used;
- a discussion of the implications for education, policy, practice or further research.

You might also want to consider what practice development initiatives you have been involved in during your professional life in the workplace. For example, have you been involved in the development of practice guidelines, an audit of current practice or developed an educational or teaching resource? Many professional journals are very much focused on engaging practitioners by publishing articles that have direct application to practice, as opposed to more esoteric articles on research methodology, so do not assume that you have to write from a very scholarly perspective. Price (2010) provides a useful article on disseminating best practice through publication in journals and urges potential writers to spend some 'thinking time' considering the purpose of the article, providing a list of different possible key messages, namely:

- to stake a claim – for example, a new approach to mentoring student practitioners;
- to educate – for example, how to investigate the body-image concerns of a person with cancer;
- to consult – for example, the challenges of making ethical decisions at the end of life;
- to challenge others – for example, what is really meant by claims of delivering spiritual care;
- to debate – for example, examining different approaches to health promotion, drawing on health beliefs and behavioural change.

(adapted from Price, 2010, p. 37)

Starting from scratch

Instead of working on a piece of work you have already done, you might want to start your article 'from scratch' and produce something on a current topic or area of professional debate. Many journals offer the chance for you to submit an opinion or 'viewpoint' piece. This is an opportunity to present a short discussion article on an issue or a reflection on something that you think might be of interest to others. Alternatively, you may wish to produce something on an aspect of clinical/professional practice – for instance, a review of a particular intervention or a case study. Whatever you decide to write about, you need to consider the following questions.

- Do I offer a new or different perspective on a topic?
- Am I clear about who my target audience is?
- Is my article underpinned by appropriate literature or research evidence?

A useful way of answering these questions is to assess what has already been published on a topic. This can be done by undertaking a quick search of relevant journal databases (as mentioned in Chapter 4). This will give you an idea of the nature, quality and quantity of published material on your possible topic and help you to consider the potential market.

WHERE DO I PUBLISH MY WORK?

Once you have decided on the content and focus of your article, you need to consider the potential market for your work. Novice writers may make the mistake of completing an article and then deciding on the journal to which they wish to submit it. This is likely to be a flawed strategy. You need to tailor the manuscript for the journal you are hoping will publish it.

ACTIVITY

Consider what factors might affect where you choose to submit your article for publication.

There are a range of factors that might influence your journal choice.

- What is the chance of acceptance? Some journals receive large numbers of unsolicited articles for consideration and so will reject a very high percentage. Wager (2005, p. 27) reminds us that nationally recognised journals such as the *Lancet* reject over 90 per cent of the papers that they receive.
- What is the length of time from submission to acceptance, and from acceptance to publication? You may wish to get something into print fairly quickly due to its topicality.
- Who is the target audience? (Is it the academic or research community? Practitioners? Professionals in a specialist field? Managers? Or multi-professional groups?)
- What are the journal's aims – and the specialist or generalist nature of the journal?
- What are the circulation and readership figures for the journal?
- Does the journal have a local or international audience?
- How frequently is the journal published?
- What is the reputation of the journal in terms of academic and professional rigour and quality?
- What is the publication medium – print or electronic?

Much of this information can be found on the website of individual journals.

Wager (2005, p. 68) proposes scanning recent issues of possible journals, '... to get an idea of the scope, coverage and hot topics. Do not rely on journal title to determine this'. Reading journals is important to assess the match between your aims and those of the other stakeholders involved. Figure 2 summarises the potentially different perspectives of all involved in what Day (2007) calls the 'writer reader chain'.

Author: Can I get my paper accepted in this journal?

Editor: Does it meet the aims of the journal and its audience?

Reviewer: Is it the right quality?

Publisher: Is the journal performing to marketing expectations?

Librarian: How can I access it – directly? Interlibrary loan? Online?

Reader: Where can I read it? Is it useful to me?

Figure 2. *The writer reader chain (Day, 2007)*

You might also want to seek the advice of colleagues or academic staff for their recommendations for suitable journals and the potential market for your work. However, the most useful step to success in achieving publication might be to contact directly the editor of the publication to which you are considering submitting your work and asking if he or she would be interested in an article on the topic, mentioning the particular argument or 'angle' you are taking. Most editors provide an email address for this purpose and our experience suggests that editors will often provide a prompt and helpful reply giving advice on currency or suitability.

THE PROCESS OF WRITING

Once you have an idea of your target journal, you need to consider issues such as the writing style and the format and length of your article. Advice on these and other specific guidance will be provided in the author guidelines or instructions that are provided by the journal. This will include instructions on layout, style, wordage and references. These author guidelines can usually be found either within a hard copy of a professional journal or on the journal's website. It is wise to invest some time in thoroughly reviewing the guidance before, during and on completion of the writing process.

The key to any successful writing, whether for publication or other reasons, is obviously a clear and coherent structure and the starting point for this is usually a well-thought-out plan.

ACTIVITY

What might be helpful to include in a plan for any article?

A plan may include points about the introduction and how you will seek to engage the audience from the outset. It should also state the key issues to be included in each section of the article with an idea of word allocation. An idea of the final conclusion to be drawn may also be helpful. Including useful references and any tables or figures, noting in which section they might appear, can also be beneficial. The more comprehensive the plan, the easier the article is likely to be to draft out, as it should enable you to remain focused on the topic and present the information in a logical format. The structure will clearly depend on the type of article being written – for example, academic convention dictates that a research article will be presented in the order:

- abstract;
- context and rationale for the research question;
- literature review;
- research methodology;

- results;
- discussion of results;
- limitations of study identified;
- conclusion summarising main points.

However, different article types will require different structures and formats – for example, an opinion piece is likely to be much shorter and may begin with an introduction, present some arguments and conclude with some suggestions on the implications of what has been discussed. More detailed advice on this is available in the further reading at the end of this chapter.

Price (2010, p. 36) discusses the importance of writers selecting a 'voice' to enable them to communicate effectively during the writing process. Figure 3 outlines the different types of writer voices that might be appropriate.

Writer voice	Typical features
Scientific/scholarly.	Significant coverage of a highly focused subject – for example, 'Measuring anxiety levels in people with newly diagnosed type 2 diabetes'. The terminology is carefully crafted and used in precise, consistent terms.
Professional/collegiate.	Typically a thematic or process coverage of subject matter. For example, 'Assessing anxiety in patients with diabetes'. There is selective use of key concepts to explain important ideas but all are explained to ensure widest access to readers.
Educational/facilitative.	Several possible foci with explanations of concepts or techniques with emphasis on 'how to' or 'how this seems or feels.' For example, 'Effective listening during a counselling interview'.
Polemical (making an argument about what should or might be).	Incisive critique is used to deconstruct what has been assumed or argued in the past. The tone is deliberate and measured, the writing analytical rather than emotive.

Figure 3. *Writer voices (adapted from Price, 2010, p. 38)*

Your voice as a writer is important as it is about getting your message across to your audience in the most accessible way.

ACTIVITY

Look through a copy of a recent journal. Pick out several different articles and read through them. As you do, try to identify the different 'voices' of the writers. Reflect on how useful the different devices are for communicating their key messages.

Whatever the 'voice', structure or topic, all writing for publication in journals needs to follow some rules to ensure it is clear to the reader. These rules include: ensuring there is a clear introduction; paragraphs that focus on one key issue or argument; a conclusion summarising findings, drawing some logical inferences from the data presented; and using short sentences, avoiding technical jargon or obscure language. The evidence base for all arguments should be explicit. You also need to consider the title – this should be as succinct as possible but should convey to the reader the main substance of the article. It is also important to bear in mind how easy the article will be to find using an internet search – it is vital that key search terms are included in the title so that it will appear high up a list of search results. The risk is that 'clever' titles are not picked up on searches because they do not describe the content of the article. Well-written abstracts are also vital to ensure the article is picked up in online searches.

Once you have a first draft, you need to put it to one side and then return to it when you have had some time to reflect on it in a considered way, and then you can start the process of editing and redrafting. Hartley (2008) provides some useful cue questions to consider when re-reading a draft.

1. Who is the text for?
2. What changes do I need to make to help the reader?
3. How can I make the script easier to follow?
4. Do I need to make big or global changes? For example, rewrite sections?
5. Do I need to make minor changes? For example, change some text slightly?

(adapted from Hartley, 2008, p. 187)

Most journals will ask you to provide an abstract to accompany the article and a list of key words. The abstract is a brief synopsis of what is in the body of the article and should provide enough information to enable the reader to decide if they wish to continue to access the whole article. Some journals ask you to use a 'structured abstract' format. A list of key words (usually around five or six) is requested to enable readers to make a quick judgement on whether the article contains material relevant to their interests. They are also designed to help the indexing services used within information databases (such as Medline) to classify papers correctly.

Ask a colleague to act as a 'critical friend' and read through your final draft to ensure that it makes sense, presents coherent arguments and that there are no obvious errors. Having been very close to the work, you may lack the objectivity needed to review it. An objective review by a friend or colleague will help to identify any obvious issues that have been omitted or not fully developed. The work must also be carefully proofread for completeness, spelling, grammatical or referencing errors prior to submission. Some but not all journals check the accuracy of all reference citations; if they don't, citation errors sometimes appear in the published version of articles. To minimise such errors, make sure that you verify references against the original documents. Do a final check to ensure the article conforms to author instructions, including providing author contact details, and then post or electronically submit it according to the instructions given. Finally, you should keep a note of when you submitted it and check in the author guidelines how soon you can expect to hear from the journal in terms of acknowledgment of receipt, rejection or feedback following peer review.

Ethical issues to consider prior to submission

As in any academic writing, there are professional and ethical issues that need to be considered to protect yourself and others. These issues come under the umbrella term of 'academic integrity'. This means having respect for the academic community in which you are participating and places upon university students, researchers, administrative and academic staff the obligation to abide by the standards governing it. These can be summarised as:

- honesty;
- confidentiality;
- fairness;
- 'ownership'.

These are also the values that are promoted, and indeed demanded, by the professional regulatory bodies in health and social care; so failure to meet these standards may mean you are also breaching your professional body's requirements.

ACTIVITY

What are the ethical issues that you need to consider, in terms of honesty, confidentiality, fairness and ownership, prior to submitting an article for publication?

Honesty is obviously a key value that must underpin all academic writing and, in particular, in the decision to publish research findings. Wood (2009) discusses the range of potential scientific misconduct by writers, which covers:

- falsification;
- fabrication;
- plagiarism;
- self-plagiarism.

The first two are essentially about dishonesty. Falsification refers to a researcher omitting or altering research processes or results, whereas fabrication is the practice of inventing data or results. The issue of plagiarism has been dealt with in Chapter 4. However, self-plagiarism is a less discussed issue. Wood (2009, p. 4) suggests that it can occur in many different forms including '… duplicate publication, data fragmentation and date augmentation'. She states the importance of avoiding reworking your own previously published articles in a different form and submitting them to other journals. She cites reasons for this as possible copyright infringement and the fact that, if you are publishing the same data, it can give undue additional weight to the findings, which is in itself a form of academic dishonesty. However, Wood does distinguish between this and the case for publishing the same study in both a research and a clinical journal to reach a different population of clinicians who are unlikely to read a research journal. She stresses the importance of annotating the article to indicate previous publication and to identify the place of first publication and ensuring agreement of both publishers.

The issue of confidentiality is obviously crucial in any writing – but particularly when writing for a wider audience. As discussed in Chapter 4, the obligation to protect the confidentiality of people and places is overriding. All individuals have a right to privacy that should not be violated without informed consent. You need to be particularly careful if you are writing about a practice or quality improvement project you have been involved in – it might be appropriate to name the institution involved but make sure that you have the written agreement of the appropriate senior managers involved. Larger organisations may have communication departments or teams who would be able to advise you on this. You also need to consider the ethical issues involved in describing practice that may be less than optimum – for example, if you were presenting audit results – and the potential impact on the morale of staff and patients/service users involved.

Fairness is about the importance of recognising and acknowledging the contribution of others to any work that you are submitting. Price (2010, p. 40) suggests that all authors should ensure that their article summarises briefly '… the conception of the project and how it was supported with idea, expertise and finance property'.

It is sensible to ensure that all stakeholders who contributed or were involved in the project are aware of your intention to publish and are in agreement with how their involvement will be acknowledged. The issues of 'authorship', that is, whose names should be included as co-authors, can be a more difficult area to address. Should everyone who has contributed to the original work be acknowledged, or just those who have contributed to the written article? The International Committee of Medical Journal Editors (ICMJ) has produced some clear guidance on this, stating that credit for authorship should be based on the following criteria.

- Substantial contributions to conception and design, acquisition of data, or analysis and interpretation of data.
- Drafting the article or revising it critically for important intellectual content.
- Final approval of the version to be published.

(ICMJ, 2009)

Other involvement should be acknowledged but not accorded authorship.

The issue of ownership – sometimes referred to as 'intellectual property' – also needs addressing. The ICMJ's criteria include 'Final approval of the version to be published'. It is therefore important to consider from whom you may be obliged to seek approval. Most universities, as part of their general student regulations, state that work undertaken as part of a course or module remains the intellectual property of the institution. This means that, on any subsequent publication, you should discuss the implications with relevant academic staff and the institution should be acknowledged in the article as, for example, 'The work described in this article was undertaken as part of MSc in Advanced Practice at the University of …'. Of course the same thing may well apply to work done while you are an employee of an organisation. If the writing has been done in work time using work resources, then the work is the intellectual property of that organisation and the organisation owns copyright. It is therefore important to check with the organisation and check your terms of employment before publishing your work.

We mentioned earlier in the chapter the possibility of inviting an academic supervisor to work with you in getting a thesis or piece of work for which you have had academic supervision into publishable form. Reviewing the ICMJ criteria, this would mean the academic supervisor should have authorship status. However, even if they were not directly involved in drafting a subsequent article, it is considered sound academic practice to discuss with your academic supervisor any consideration of publishing work generated from a dissertation and to invite them to be acknowledged as co-author. This is fair as it acknowledges their contribution in terms of the guidance and support that you received in getting the dissertation into a robust form. Similarly, no academic supervisor should publish any part of your work without your involvement and agreement.

You also need to consider copyright issues if you are including any diagrams or tables in your article. If an original figure or table is used intact, without any changes made, permission to reproduce the work needs to be sought from the copyright holder. This also applies to quoting large sections of text, usually more than 400 words long. You should always seek advice from the editor on this prior to inclusion.

Finally, you must ensure that you only submit the article to one journal at a time. Indeed, many journals now ask you to sign a statement confirming that the work has not been previously published elsewhere or submitted for consideration elsewhere. Of course, if the work is rejected, you may then legitimately submit it to another journal for consideration.

COPING WITH REJECTION OR REQUESTS TO REVISE

Manuscripts submitted to journals will usually go through the review process. As described in Chapter 4, this is the process whereby an unbiased, independent, critical assessment of the work is undertaken. First this is carried out by the editor and the article is then sent off for peer review, usually to two reviewers. These reviewers will usually be experts in their field who are not part of the editorial staff. Although its actual value has been widely debated (Hartley, 2008, p. 151), peer review helps editors decide on a manuscript's suitability and helps authors to improve the quality of the article.

There are a number of possible outcomes for your submitted article. These are:

- outright rejection;
- major revision needed prior to resubmission;
- minor revisions needed prior to resubmission;
- acceptance.

It is very unusual to have your work accepted without any need for any revision or changes. In fact, having an article rejected is a common experience for most writers – novice or experienced. Indeed, Belcher (2009, p. 7) states that many Nobel Prize winners have had early versions of their award-winning work rejected by editors. It has been estimated that editors immediately reject between 10 and 15 per cent of submitted articles, without ever sending them through the peer review process (Belcher, 2009, p. 69).

ACTIVITY

Why do you think that so many submitted articles are rejected even before the peer review process?

Rejections do not necessarily mean that the quality of your writing is poor. It may be a question of the topicality of the subject matter – for example, it might be that there has already been a recently published article on the topic. Alternatively, it may be that the editor of the journal feels that the topic has been overrepresented in recent times, or it may be that the topic itself is no longer current. It could also be that the subject matter is too narrow in its scope and would not interest enough readers – this may particularly apply to very specialist subjects that need to be targeted by the writer to a special journal audience. Editors may also reject articles that do not adhere to the instructions to authors that all journals provide.

ACTIVITY

List some of the reasons you think that a reviewer may reject a submitted article.

Reasons for rejections by a reviewer could include:

- not scholarly enough – too basic in its analysis and assumptions or lacks adequate reference to current literature;
- not sufficiently original – it does not add to the body of knowledge in its field;
- poor writing style or structure – over-complex language, for example, or an unbalanced use of a limited word count;
- theoretically or methodologically flawed;
- no arguments presented – or arguments not presented clearly;
- ethical considerations not adequately addressed.

Even if the work has been rejected outright by one journal, it may well be accepted by another publication. In the interests of transparency, even if the article is rejected outright, most journal editors will send authors some feedback from the reviewers in either complete or summarised form. Of course, you need to carefully and honestly review the comments received and ask yourself if the rejection is due to the quality of the work – in which case it is unlikely to be accepted elsewhere – or if it is more about the suitability for that particular journal's readership.

Thomson (2005) suggests putting any rejection or revision letter away for 48 hours after receipt before returning to it and carefully considering the comments. She urges the aspiring writer to 'Remember that the referees are trying to improve your paper so that it can be published …'. Clearly, you will need to assess what needs to be done and undertake the revision promptly and if, for any reason, you decide not to make some of the recommended alterations, it is usually acceptable to enter into a dialogue with the editor to discuss your justification for this. Ignoring guidance and just resubmitting without discussing it with the editor is likely to lead to further rejection. Belcher (2009) goes so far as urging the writer to make the editor 'your friend'. This means sticking to deadlines, completing documentation fully and accurately, supplying the finished paper precisely to specifications, and not altering proofs other than correcting typographical errors.

SUPPORT FOR WRITING

A well-known writer is alleged to have said 'Writing is easy. All you have to do is sit down at a typewriter and open a vein!' (anonymous, cited in Steinert et al., 2008). For some writers, this provides an accurate analogy for the potentially painful process of producing an article. However, there is evidence that initiatives to support novice writers can be helpful. The literature demonstrates the value of a range of support mechanisms including writing groups (Steinert et al., 2008), writing coaches (Baldwin and Chandler, 2002), journal clubs (Kleinpell, 2002), support from academic staff (Staudt et al., 2003) and writing workshops (Murray, 2002).

Personally, we would advocate the role of collaborative writing for supporting the novice writer. This is the process when two or more authors combine efforts to develop a single writing project (Keen, 2006, p. 386). It is likely that this will lead to a better-quality article. Indeed, Bahr and Zemon (2000) cited research that showed that papers with multiple authors are published more frequently, require less revision and receive more citations. Certainly we have found co-authorship to be a positive and enriching experience, facilitating the sharing of expertise and resources. In addition to providing emotional support, team loyalty often provides the 'spur' needed to meet deadlines. However, there is also a need to consider potential areas of conflict, which could include:

- differing writing styles;
- agreeing on the key message/content of article;
- the order of author names on publication;
- timescales for drafts and completion;
- agreeing different levels of contribution to the writing or researching process.

It is possible to overcome these conflicts provided there is open and honest dialogue about potentially differing expectations. There are different models of collaborative writing such as, for example, where one writer produces a first draft and the second person is responsible for editing and strengthening the article. A different approach may be to divide the work up into sections for different authors. However, someone needs to oversee the finished product to ensure that a seamless and coherent finished article is produced.

ACTIVITY

Consider colleagues who might be interested in collaborating on a writing project with you. Find out if there is any other support for writers available either in your workplace or in your university.

OTHER TYPES OF SCHOLARLY ACTIVITY

Even if you feel overwhelmed by the idea of submitting an article for publication, there are other ways you might consider disseminating work that you have undertaken. These could include the following.

Presenting a conference poster

This is where you present findings from a project, research or quality-improvement initiatives in poster format. You will usually be required to attend the conference and be available to stand with your poster to discuss and provide additional information as requested by delegates. Hartley (2008, p. 111) provides a nice summary of key issues to consider when developing a poster.

Presenting a paper at a conference

This may seem daunting but many health and social care professionals will regularly undertake teaching sessions or presentations as part of their work, so this is just the next step. Co-presenting with a colleague may be a less intimidating way to start as a presenter. Once you have summarised your work into a presentation format, it should be relatively easy to 'work this up' into a manuscript format for publication.

Leading a workshop or 'break out' session at a conference

This will be with a smaller number of delegates than presenting a key paper and may help to boost confidence in your presentation skills.

Writing a book review for a journal

Most journals provide brief synopses of recently published texts and material, giving a short evaluation of the strengths and limitations of the work. These are relatively easy to do and usually brief – about 100 to 200 words – and require you to provide an informed opinion on a recent book. It is worth contacting an editor to see if you can join their database of book reviewers, letting them know your areas of professional interest and expertise. Most journals do not accept unsolicited book reviews.

Writing a letter to an editor for publication

Peer-reviewed journals usually welcome letters from readers, particularly those that offer some critique of, or add to an argument raised by, a recent published article.

All of the above can be considered as 'scholarly' activity as they have the potential to play an important part in the development of the body of knowledge for the health and social care community, generating debate and getting professionals to consider the evidence base for their practice. However, they are also important steps in inspiring you to maximise your knowledge and skills as an expert practitioner who has gained some 'mastery' in your specialist field.

SUMMARY

This chapter has taken you through the process of getting an article published. Figure 4 summarises the stages outlined.

Process summary:

- Identify topic.
- Consider target audience.
- Consider issues around acknowledgements, consent and authorship and seek advice if needed.
- Select appropriate journal – consider approaching editor to see if article idea would be of interest.
- Read the chosen journal for article style.
- Read and keep referring to the journal instructions for authors.
- Plan the structure and outline.
- Draft and carefully proofread, especially references.
- Check any copyright permission is obtained.
- Get critical friend to review prior to submission.
- Check requirements for abstract, key words and title page.
- Submit to one journal only.
- Wait patiently.
- Make any recommended changes if accepted with revision.
- Resubmit amended manuscript.

Figure 4. *The process of getting an article published (adapted from Keen, 2006)*

In summary, it is clear that writing for publication requires a high investment in terms of time and energy, but has the potential for high personal and professional rewards for the Master's level student.

Critical reflection	
Identify at least three things that you have learned from this chapter.	1. 2. 3.
How do you plan to use this knowledge?	1. 2. 3.

How will you evaluate the effectiveness of your plan?	1.
	2.
	3.
What further knowledge and evidence do you need?	1.
	2.
	3.

FURTHER READING

Wager, E. (2005) *Getting Research Published: An A to Z of Publication Strategy*. Oxford: Radcliffe Publishing
This book provides a useful and accessible guide to getting biomedical and health care research published.

Webb, C. (2008) *Writing for Publication: An Easy to Follow Guide for any Nurse Thinking of Publishing Their Work*. Wiley-Blackwell.
www.nurseauthoreditor.com/WritingforPublicationbooklet2008.pdf
This is a free downloadable guide that takes the reader through the process of preparing an article for publication and, in particular, it gives guidance on the structure and style of different types of journal articles.

7

APPLYING POSTGRADUATE KNOWLEDGE AND SKILLS IN THE WORKPLACE

This chapter covers the following key issues:

- the concept of employability and employability assets;
- the importance of critical thinking, decision-making and problem-solving in the workplace;
- the importance of postgraduate skills in service development and doing things differently;
- the importance of postgraduate skills in professional practice;
- the importance of postgraduate skills in leadership roles;
- the importance of postgraduate skills when working in a patient-led, consumerist health and social care service.

By the end of this chapter you should be able to:

- discuss the importance of postgraduate skills in the workplace;
- describe the concept of employability and employability assets;
- demonstrate an awareness of the importance of postgraduate skills in relation to decision-making and problem-solving, service development, professional practice, leadership and working in the current context of health and social care services.

INTRODUCTION

As early as 1996 the American Association of Colleges of Nursing (AACN) reported general agreement that Master's education is achieving notable goals, including the development of refined analytical skills, broad-based perspectives, enhanced abilities to articulate viewpoints and positions, clearer ability to connect theory to practice, and enhanced skills in a specific profession (AACN, 1996). They cited research (Conrad, Howard and Miller, 1993) that gave strong support to the important role that graduate education plays in developing a cadre of skilled professionals who make important contributions to the health, education, business, political and social structure of the United States. As a result, and in recognition of this, career progression is increasingly linked to academic achievements, with an increasing number of health and social care practitioners pursuing Master's and even doctoral levels of study. Having a definable knowledge base is important. For nursing and allied health professions, what is increasingly under the microscope is the knowledge base for the profession and what it is that expedites the ways in which professionals provide care and influence patient outcomes (Jasper, 2006). Education, the means to improve the knowledge base and importantly its application across health and social care professions, is therefore about enabling and improving the individual's autonomy, control and accountability in a given practice situation and such skills are very important in the workplace. This chapter will examine why postgraduate skills and knowledge are essential to the workplace and examine this in the context of employability and quality assurance.

KNOWLEDGE AND SKILLS DEVELOPMENT IN MASTER'S EDUCATION

We will begin by reflecting on the knowledge and skills that Master's level education develops. In Chapter 1 we identified the Master's level attributes from the QAA that are necessary for employment (QAA, 2010). They state that, typically, holders of a Master's will have:

the qualities and transferable skills necessary for employment requiring:

- the exercise of initiative and personal responsibility;
- decision-making in complex and unpredictable situations; and
- the independent learning ability required for continuing professional development.

ACTIVITY

Consider your current role or the role that you aspire to move to once you have completed your Master's qualification. Why are the three QAA attributes important in that role? Will improving your skills in this area make you more likely to be successful in the role, or more likely to gain 'promotion' within your field?

The concept of 'employability'

The concept of employability is a very important one for anybody wishing to undertake further study in order to increase their career aspirations. There is a national policy focus on what is described as the 'skills agenda' following the Leitch Review of Skills, published in 2006, which highlighted that employability skills are essential not only to business competitiveness but also to prosperity and fairness (Maxwell *et al.*, 2009). But what are the skills that employers are looking for in graduates and what do we mean by employability? Employability is a difficult concept to define succinctly and comprehensively (Lees, 2002). Very simply, employability is about having the capability to gain initial employment, maintain employment and obtain new employment if required. According to a report authored by Hillage and Pollard (1998, p. 1), for the individual, employability depends on:

- their assets in terms of the knowledge, skills and attitudes they possess;
- the way they use and deploy those assets;
- the way they present them to employers;
- and, crucially, the context (for example, personal circumstances and labour market environment) within which they work.

The first two of these elements warrant further consideration.

Employability assets

An individual's 'employability assets' comprise their knowledge (i.e., what they know), skills (what they do with what they know) and attitudes (how they do it).

ACTIVITY

Think about your job or profession. What knowledge (what you know); which skills (what you do with what you know); and what attitudes (how you do it) are important for you to progress in your career?

Those of you working in the NHS will have recognised the elements here that make up the NHS Knowledge and Skills Framework (KSF) (DH, 2004). Although the NHS Staff Council has developed a simplified KSF that is intended to be easier to use in practice, the original principles still underpin the process of appraisal and development review, and the application of these elements has been described in the KSF as the assets that make up 'competence'.

Thinking more closely about these assets, it may be that you are able to distinguish between:

- **baseline assets** such as basic skills and essential personal attributes (such as reliability and integrity);

- **intermediate assets** such as occupational specific skills (at all levels), generic or key skills (such as communication and problem-solving) and key personal attributes (such as motivation and initiative); and
- **high-level assets** involving skills that help contribute to organisational performance (such as teamworking, self-management, financial awareness and leadership).

(adapted from Hillage and Pollard,1998)

ACTIVITY

For those of you working within the NHS:

- Access the summary descriptions of the KSF Core Dimensions at **www.nhsemployers. org/SiteCollectionDocuments/Summary_KSF_core_dim_fb131110.docx**
- Examine the Core Dimensions and identify the levels at which you feel Master's level assets apply.

For those working outside the NHS, it might be useful to examine the competency framework used by your employer or the essential and desirable attributes described on your job description and undertake the same exercise.

Deployment

Hillage and Pollard (1998) also argue that assets are a linked set of abilities that include career management skills. They state that these are commonly identified as self-awareness (including the ability to recognise one's own occupational interests and abilities), opportunity awareness (knowing what work opportunities exist and their entry requirements, including labour-market knowledge), decision-making skills (to develop a strategy of getting from where you are to where you want to be) and transition skills. Transition skills can be about issues like possessing job-search skills in order to find suitable jobs, which might include networking (formal and informal) and having a strategic approach to employment and so being adaptable and flexible, but this can also be about recognising transferable skills and having the confidence to try them out in new arenas. This demonstrates an important interrelationship between assets and deployment. The extent to which an individual is aware of what they possess in terms of knowledge, skills and attitudes and their relevance to the employment opportunities available may affect their willingness to undertake training and other activities designed to upgrade their skills. Critical thinking and reflection are key to this.

Critical thinking and employment

Why is critical thinking important to both professionals and employers? Critical thinking is clearly not restricted to the world of academia. It is a skill used in a variety of situations in that it enables us to make informed decisions about events and issues in our everyday life – such as making choices about our lifestyle or attempting to understand the behaviour of others. Critical thinking therefore appears to be a desirable characteristic for all human beings in that it is associated with tolerance and rationale decision-making. Taylor (2000) suggests that it '… turns an unconsidered life to one that is consciously aware, self-potentiating and purposeful' (Taylor, 2000, p. 10).

Others have suggested that critical thinking is fundamental to the survival of a democratic way of life (Ennis, 1996, p. 17) and is associated with making fair collective decisions. Certainly oppressive regimes have been implicated in the oppression of academics and students in universities, presumably fearing the effects of those who can think critically about moral, ethical and social trends. Daly (1998, p. 232) goes as far as suggesting that the ability of a society to make rational, informed and tolerant decisions is proportionate to the critical thinking abilities of individuals in a democracy.

The notion of critical thinkers being crucial in health and social care is discussed by Fook and Gardner (2007). They suggest that critical reflection:

> … involves the unsettling and examination of fundamental (socially dominant and often hidden) individually held assumptions about the social world, in order to enable a reworking of these and associated actions for changed professional practice.
>
> (Fook and Gardner, 2007, p. 21)

In other words, health and social care professionals need critical thinking skills in order to challenge current ideologies and practices with a view to achieving better practice. This seems particularly important in the current health and social care environment with some of the pressures and challenges facing professionals today, in particular the tensions between value-based practice as espoused by professional ethical codes, and the technical, economic and outcome-focused organisations where practice occurs. The increasing complexity of the care environment and the need to protect and risk-manage services mean the increasing need to unsettle dominant/fundamental theories in current practice to offer the potential for improved practice.

ACTIVITY

Reflect on your current job or profession. In what ways has the environment increased in complexity over the past decade? You may want to consider issues of:

- 'tasks' undertaken;
- skills required;
- service-user or 'consumer' expectations;
- access to information;
- the increased requirement for collaborative working across professional and service user groups.

It has been argued that the need for high-level clinical reasoning, for example, arises from the increasingly high level of complexity seen when dealing with the health and health deficits of human beings as complex holistic organisms, who compromise individual ontological constructs, perspectives, abilities, levels of physical and cognitive functioning, expectations, responses and coping mechanisms (Daly, 1998). It is thus essential for health and social care practitioners to consider both technical rational aspects of care alongside the humanistic aspects of care that extend beyond simple judgement.

There is therefore a strong relationship between decision-making skills and the ability to think critically. An early piece of work by Girot (1995) acknowledged that there was a growing recognition of the importance of critical thinking as an essential requirement for nurses to engage in safe, competent and autonomous practice. Certainly the seminal work of Benner (1984) based on Dreyfus' model of skills acquisition, suggests that practitioners move through five cognitive stages to become an expert nurse. The novice relies on abstract principles and the application of rules to guide their practice. However, the expert performer no longer relies on analytical principles to connect her or his understanding of the situation to an appropriate action. The expert nurse, with an enormous background of experience, now has an intuitive grasp of each situation and makes an accurate assessment of the problem. This ability to recognise context, without conscious consideration of a large range of unfruitful, alternative diagnoses and solutions, is clearly allied to the skills of the critical thinker. Indeed, a recent Department of Health (DH, 2008) document suggested that clinicians increasingly were:

- dealing with complexity and managing uncertainty;
- working with patients to take legitimate risks and effectively managing risk by providing information alongside professional judgment to maximise patient independence and choice;
- grasping clinical situations intuitively based on a deep, tacit understanding of their area of practice.

(DH, 2008, p. 14)

It could also be argued that the ability to apply critical thinking to clinical decision-making is what distinguishes professionals from the non-professional assistant worker. This is of particular relevance when we consider the current developments around the role of the assistant practitioner in health and social care. This was brought sharply into focus by the press release on the publication of care standards for assistant practitioners by Skills for Health in November 2009:

The Assistant Practitioner would be able to deliver elements of health and social care and undertake clinical work in domains that have previously only been within the remit of registered professionals. The Assistant Practitioner may transcend professional boundaries.

(Skills for Health, 2009, p. 2)

It may be that the role of critical thinking and decision-making skills in practice is a key element in any debate around the role and scope of the assistant practitioner in health and social care in the future.

PROBLEM-SOLVING AND DECISION-MAKING

The features of the cognitive processes involved in problem-solving and decision-making are directed towards acquiring and evaluating data in order to make decisions and judgements about problems and appropriate solutions. In health and social care settings multiple actions and interactions are exemplified for the purpose of gathering information by consulting and collaborating with members of the multidisciplinary team, reading case notes, observations and assessments in order to undertake a systematic physical assessment and evaluate a service user's needs. Processes involving the collection, organisation and assimilation of written and verbal information are undertaken to assist decision-making, problem-solving and critical thinking in both clinical arenas (Fairly and Closs, 2006) and non-clinical health and social care settings.

The process of decision-making and, integral to this, the ability to solve problems, are key skills to be developed within Master's level courses and can be described as critical thinking in action. While on first consideration it might be perceived that the consequences of decisions by professionals impact on the recipients of services, it is important to point out that decisions are made all the time that also affect the team members within any service organisation. So consideration of problem-solving and decision-making must take into account the needs of all those affected, not simply those who access services.

ACTIVITY

1. Think about your workplace. Identify decisions that have been made recently that have affected you or members of your team. You may want to consider issues of deployment or working practices.
2. What decisions have been made that have a direct impact on the client group or individual service recipients?

Models and methods of decision-making and problem-solving

There are many theoretical approaches or models of problem-solving and decision-making that lead the individual through a process or number of steps in an attempt to improve their skills. These include a traditional problem-solving seven-step model.

1. Identify the problem.
2. Gather data to analyse the causes and consequences of the problem.
3. Explore alternative approaches.
4. Evaluate the alternatives.

5. Select the appropriate solution.
6. Implement the appropriate solution.
7. Evaluate the results.

In this model the decision is made at Step 5.

There is also the managerially-based model:

1. Set objectives.
2. Search for alternatives.
3. Evaluate alternatives.
4. Choose.
5. Implement.
6. Follow up and control.

In this model the decision is made at Step 4.

(Marquis and Huston, 2008, p. 26)

Often individuals may try to make decisions without being completely clear about the goals, and they can fail because decisions have to be made using available knowledge and information. This is where the value of having developed Master's level skills can be identified.

ACTIVITY

Consider the following list of Master's level attributes from the QAA and think about the way in which the stages of the decision-making process described in one of the models above match the attributes below.

Master's degrees are awarded to students who have demonstrated:	The stages of decision-making
i. a systematic understanding of knowledge, and a critical awareness of current problems and/or new insights, much of which is at, or informed by, the forefront of their academic discipline, field of study, or area of professional practice;	
ii. a comprehensive understanding of techniques applicable to their own research or advanced scholarship;	

iii. originality in the application of knowledge, together with a practical understanding of how established techniques of research and enquiry are used to create and interpret knowledge in the discipline;	
iv. conceptual understanding that enables the student: • to evaluate critically current research and advanced scholarship in the discipline; and • to evaluate methodologies and develop critiques of them and, where appropriate, to propose new hypotheses.	

Typically, holders of the qualification will be able to:	**The stages of decision-making**
a. deal with complex issues both systematically and creatively, make sound judgements in the absence of complete data, and communicate their conclusions clearly to specialist and non-specialist audiences;	
b. demonstrate self-direction and originality in tackling and solving problems, and act autonomously in planning and implementing tasks at a professional or equivalent level;	
c. continue to advance their knowledge and understanding, and to develop new skills to a high level;	
and will have:	
d. the qualities and transferable skills necessary for employment requiring: • the exercise of initiative and personal responsibility; • decision-making in complex and unpredictable situations; and • the independent learning ability required for continuing professional development.	

Types of decision

It is true to say that not all types of decisions are the same. Marquis and Huston (2008) defined three types of decision as routine, urgent and considered, arguing that each of these takes a different approach and skill. A routine decision is one that usually does not cause difficulty or disagreement, an urgent decision has an immediate and informed response, and considered decisions are often the most difficult, with input from a number of different people, each of whom may be affected by the decision made and who have the expectation, if not the right, to be involved.

ACTIVITY

Can you identify decisions in your workplace that could be categorised as routine or urgent?

Considered decision-making

Considered decisions within a care situation will normally entail shared or collaborative decision-making (Hayes and Llewellyn, 2010) and it is essential that a stepped approach to the consideration of options and outcomes is adopted. It is also important to recognise that individual decisions are based on the individual's own value system and that, regardless of how objective the criteria used are, value judgements will always play a part (Marquis and Huston, 2008). Value judgements can be referred to as intuition based on past experiences and professionalism but it is essential to think carefully about the decisions made and justify them according to objective criteria. Developing self-awareness and reflective practice is an important element in problem-solving outcomes.

There are therefore a number of critical elements in problem-solving and decision-making that should always be considered.

- It is essential that decisions have a clear objective.
- Decisions are based on knowledge and so the acquisition of knowledge and information is a clear and important need (for both care professionals and clients).
- As problem-solvers gather information it must be recognised that preference is not mistaken for fact. This is why it is so important that many alternatives are generated in the decision-making process and also that ethical decision-making is considered (see below).

Ethical decision-making

Consideration of ethical issues is also important. This is because of the importance of taking time to consider our own personal values and the impact they may have on our practice, as well as on those involved as decision-makers or individuals who will be affected by the consequences of the decision.

By considering the ethics of a decision we are acknowledging that there is a moral code that underpins practice, based on 'the primary principle of obligation embodied in the concepts of service to people and respect for human life' (Carper, 1978, p. 17). In ambiguous situations, it may be difficult to predict the consequences of one's actions and the moral context of making difficult personal choices, determining what is good and bad or what ought to be done in a situation, must be considered (Hayes and Llewellyn, 2010). Reflective thinking refers to the capacity to develop critical consideration of one's own worldview and its relationship to the worldview of others. It is the ability to transcend preconceptions, prejudices and frames of reference and it underlies the capacity to learn from others and from experience (Warn and Tranter, 2001).

Decision-making must therefore reflect the four ethical principles as first discussed by Beauchamp and Childress (2001).

- **Autonomy** – the right of a person (that is, both service users and the professional as an employee) to make their own decisions and direct their life.
- **Beneficence** – the responsibility of doing good and so providing benefit or beneficial treatment/care to the recipient of services or individuals you are working with.
- **Non-maleficence** – the responsibility of avoiding harm to the person (fellow employees or clients).
- **Justice** – the responsibility to be equitable and fair in the way we treat all others.

(adapted from Hayes and Llewellyn, 2010)

ACTIVITY

Consider again the list of Master's level attributes from the QAA. How do these attributes enable the development of these ethical principles?

- Autonomy.
- Beneficence.
- Non-maleficence.
- Justice?

Writers (Alfaro-Lefevre, 1995, and Daly, 1998) also talk about effective clinical judgements as reasoning strategies that can arguably be applied in a number of arenas not solely confined to clinical ones. Daly talks about 'precise, disciplined thinking that enhances accuracy and depth of data collection' in order to identify the issues at hand (Daly, 1998, p. 327). To achieve this there are principles that should be followed such as:

- acquiring a factual knowledge base;
- using models as reasoning frameworks (such as the nursing process);
- exercising accountability in the recognition of limitations;
- the importance of prioritising one's reasoning and actions.

THE IMPORTANCE OF POSTGRADUATE SKILLS IN SERVICE DEVELOPMENT OR IN DOING THINGS DIFFERENTLY

Sometimes the outcome of decision-making at service level is actually a recognition of the need to do things differently. Master's level working can engender this by encouraging people to question established knowledge, and therefore promoting a culture of open and intelligent debate that stimulates innovation and new approaches to tackling difficult challenges.

Service improvement is an important element of practice in health and social care organisations and there are different aspects to the process of improving services. In 2007 the NHS Institute for Innovation and Improvement (NHSI, 2007a) published a series of improvement leaders' guides aimed at developing sustained service improvement across the NHS. Although the Institute was replaced by a new body in April 2013, the work of improvement continues. The specific areas the Institute focused on in their guides included:

- improving knowledge and skills;
- managing the human dimensions of change;
- building and nurturing an improvement culture;
- evaluation improvement;
- leading improvements;
- involving patients and carers;
- process mapping, analysis and redesign;
- measurement for improvement;
- matching capacity and demand;
- redesigning roles.

ACTIVITY

Reflecting on the areas listed above, how might your Master's course or a Master's level qualification prepare you to undertake service development and change?

Undertaking a Master's course may enable you to lead service development (and leadership will be discussed in more detail below) and/or enable you to undertake extended roles or do things differently with your services. Such extended roles, when supported by educational development, have been seen to give real benefits for service users, team members and individual staff by:

- improving access to care, diagnosis and treatment;
- improving quality;
- reducing waiting lists;

- managing ever-increasing workloads;
- job satisfaction;
- career development.

(NHS Institute for Innovation and Improvement (NHSI), 2007b)

As an example, advanced practitioner (AP) roles within nursing, which have been essentially service driven, have been researched and identified as having a positive impact on patient care and service delivery in their Trusts (Shapiro and the University of York, 2009). As Master's graduates, advanced practitioners have demonstrated:

- the capacity to work beyond their base profession;
- being 'advanced' practitioners as opposed to highly skilled nurses, midwives or Allied Health Professionals;
- improving activity and service delivery;
- increasing workforce productivity by improving training and support for other staff, including junior medical staff and staff from partner organisations (for example, nursing homes);
- there was a noticeable increase in confidence in relation to communication with management colleagues.

(Shapiro and the University of York, 2009)

ACTIVITY

Reflecting on the QAA attributes for Master's level qualification, why would doing a Master's degree lead to increased confidence?

POSTGRADUATE SKILLS AND PROFESSIONAL PRACTICE

Earlier it was suggested that it is possible to argue that the ability to apply critical thinking to clinical decision-making in practice is what distinguishes professionals from the non-professional assistant worker. But what is professional practice? There are many theories of professionalism (Johnson, 1972) but a common way to define a group as a profession is to describe it as based on the creation and defence of a specialist body of knowledge, typically based on formal university qualifications; the establishment of control over a specialised client market and exclusion of competitor groups from that market; the establishment of control over professional work practice, responsibilities and obligations while resisting control from managerial or bureaucratic staff (Bilton *et al.*, 2002, p. 426).

Reflect briefly on Bilton *et al.*'s description of professionalism. Consider your own professional group. How does your understanding of your profession fit with Bilton's description? You may wish to consider issues such as:

- academic qualifications;
- research in your field;
- professional body regulation;
- the 'place' of 'unregistered' staff.

Think also about the QAA Master's level attributes. How do they engender membership of a profession?

At a fundamental level professional practice is about what individuals in health and social care do as a result of being registered with a professional body; for example in nursing this is the Nursing and Midwifery Council (NMC) and for social workers it is the Health and Care Professions Council (HCPC).

Expectations of professional behaviour come from:

- professional bodies;
- legal regulation;
- policy directives;
- employers who set boundaries and expectations through employment rules and guidance and policy;
- service users and carers who have expectations or make certain demands of professionals.

Thinking about Johnson's assertions, what is the particular body of knowledge that professionals working in health and social care settings 'create and defend' and what part does education play in this? In nursing terms it may be useful to return to Benner's expert practitioner (Benner, 1984). In her model of professional development Benner describes a process of skills development titled 'From novice to expert' and identifies five stages through which nurses pass in moving from being a new recruit in the profession to reaching expertise as a practitioner. Jasper (2006) used Benner's work and combined it with that of Robinson *et al.* (2003) to describe the expert practitioner as someone who:

- functions from an intuitive base;
- has developed a comprehensive knowledge base;
- is self-directed and flexible and innovative;
- operates from a deep understanding of a total situation to resolve complex issues;
- works collaboratively with other health care team providers;

- actively and positively influences the team, fosters critical thinking in others and forms mentoring relationships with other nurses;
- participates in and leads activities that improve systems for quality patient care;
- serves as a change agent to challenge themselves and others.

(adapted from Jasper, 2006, p. 22)

ACTIVITY

1. What is intuition?
2. Why would a Master's course enable intuitive practice?

It therefore appears from Jasper's work that expert practitioners, with a comprehensive knowledge base and assets such as innovation and flexibility, are in a key place to undertake leadership roles in practice. The Master's graduate should demonstrate certain personal qualities and professional behaviours such as assertiveness, the responsibility to engage in professional activities and advocacy for change. Professionals thus may rely on the Master's-prepared individuals to participate actively in the profession and exert leadership, not only within the profession but also across the health and social care system.

Postgraduate skills and leadership

Much has been written about leadership and it is argued that, while good management brings a degree of consistency and order, leadership skill contributes to the achievement of plans by motivating and inspiring individuals to keep up with the direction needed and enables individuals to both cope with and enable change (Kotter, 2001). Beyond the management tasks of organising and staffing, delegating duties and responsibilities, leaders communicate direction to the staff, who can then create 'coalitions' that understand the vision or direction of the organisation and, through commitment to it, move the agenda on (Kotter, 2001, p. 86).

Much leadership research has until recently been based within the military context, which tends to require inspirational leaders who could persuade individuals to sacrifice even their life for the greater good. These so-called 'great man theories' were based on the personality traits of high-energy, charismatic extroverts. But, in organisations where leadership focuses on one person, others may think that whatever is wrong will be fixed by the leader and do not consider or look for solutions of their own (Mintzberg, 1996). Much human potential is therefore lost.

This is demonstrated by two very different types of manager/leader as described by Burns (1978). Transactional leaders direct individuals to a certain outcome. The aim is to deliver certain results and is comparable to many task-oriented management theories. However, transformational leadership is concerned with enabling others through identifying common goals and vision. Unlike the 'great men' models, transformational leaders give away their power, they serve others and, in doing so, enable others to lead themselves. Transformational leaders do not want to make mini-replicas of themselves but celebrate the difference of people as individuals (Alimo-Metcalfe, 2003). They acknowledge that others see the world differently and want to release an individual's potential to find different solutions to issues within the workplace. This requires trust, removing barriers to communicating and also welcoming challenge, which may result in innovative solutions to old problems and has positive outcomes for all, as the greatest asset of any organisation – its workforce – is able or rather 'enabled' to release its full potential.

ACTIVITY

Consider the employability assets described by Hillage and Potter (1996) earlier in this chapter.

- **'Baseline assets'** such as basic skills and essential personal attributes (such as reliability and integrity).
- **'Intermediate assets'** such as occupational-specific skills (at all levels), generic or key skills (such as communication and problem-solving) and key personal attributes (such as motivation and initiative).
- **'High-level assets'** involving skills that help contribute to organisational performance (such as teamworking, self-management and financial awareness).

How would these assets enable an individual 'leader' to release the potential of the workforce to its full potential?

While it is apparent that leadership characteristics are variable and applicable differently in different contexts, three clusters or qualities have been identified by the Institute for Innovation and Improvement within their NHS Leadership Qualities Framework (NHSI, 2007c). These are:

- **Personal qualities**, which includes: self belief, self awareness, self management, drive for improvement and personal integrity;
- **Setting direction**, which includes: seizing the future, intellectual flexibility, broad scanning, political astuteness and drive for results;
- and **delivering the service** which includes: leading change through people, holding to account, empowering others, effective and strategic influencing and collaborative working.

(NHSI, 2007c)

ACTIVITY

Visit **www.nhsleadershipqualities.nhs.uk**

1. Consider how the Master's level attributes that you will develop on your course can be applied within these qualities.
2. Also, as you progress though your Master's course, you may want to consider how you could focus on the development of these skills through the assignments that you need to complete or through your long project or research. An example may be fulfilling an extended study that focuses on leading a change project.

POSTGRADUATE SKILLS IN A 'PATIENT-LED', 'CONSUMERIST' SOCIETY

The importance of Master's level skills in our modern society and in the current context of health and social care services needs to be acknowledged. As discussed by Crinson (2008), from 2001 the last Labour government's policy for health and social care increasingly embraced the 'choice' agenda. This proposed the wrapping together of the delivery of public services with consumerism, and this ideology has further strengthened under the Coalition government elected in 2010 with the publication of the White Paper *Equity and Excellence: Liberating the NHS* (DH, 2010). Services have historically developed according to a welfarist model, where welfare professionals have identified needs and then provided services to address these needs. An increase in consumerism and consumer rights has led to a shift in ideology and power, with greater emphasis on user and carer involvement in care and individual assessment of need and care packages tailored to meet those needs (Hayes and Llewellyn, 2010). Thus there is a shift from service-led provision to needs-led care, with the care recipient at the centre of the decision-making process.

Such 'consumer power' forges a demand-led market within a neoliberal market economy that urges an opening up of public sector services to the exercise of service user choice (Crinson, 2008). In this context it is argued that consumerism and choice will lead to improved quality.

ACTIVITY

What are the challenges that consumerism and choice pose for the professional working in health and social care?

Consumerism and choice offer the professional working in health and social care a number of challenges. This shift in ideology and balance of provision of services has led to a need for more collaborative and partnership working between the different professional groups involved in the delivery of health and social care, and with service users and carers (Hayes and Llewellyn, 2010), and collaborative working in this way presents a number of challenges, not least in reference to the concept of co-production, where service users are seen as active contributors to every stage of their care. Co-production emphasises that people are not passive recipients of services and have assets and expertise that can help improve services. Therefore, it can potentially transform the way of thinking about power, resources, partnerships, risks and outcomes, and implies that there is not an off-the-shelf model of service provision or a single 'magic solution'. It focuses on the empowerment of both users and providers to act as partners in the care process – co-production means involving citizens in collaborative relationships with more empowered frontline staff who are able and confident to share power and accept user expertise. It requires the creation of new structures, regulatory and commissioning practices and financial streams which are necessary to embed co-production as a long-term rather than an *ad hoc* solution; and it requires learning from existing international case studies of co-production while recognising that the contribution of initiatives reflecting local needs is important (Hayes and Llewellyn 2010).

Essentially, then, this new paradigm of service-led or consumer-led health and social care changes the rules for professionals and demands far greater collaboration and joint working. It also requires a heightened focus on equity as the promotion of a choice agenda raises important questions with regard to access. There have been concerns about the 'inverse care law' (Tudor Hart, 2006) where there is a greater utilisation of care resources by the middle classes who have the social, educational and economic capital to pursue their needs when compared with the lower socio-economic classes who do not access care to the same extent. Thus unequal health-seeking behaviours compound inequities of health and social care access (Crinson, 2008).

ACTIVITY

1. Why is it important for health and social care professionals to be educated to Master's level in a 'patient-led' public sector? List at least eight assets or attributes.
2. Once you have identified your assets or attributes, consider how you could evidence these to a potential employer at interview.

SUMMARY

This chapter has considered the application of postgraduate knowledge and skills in the workplace. The concepts of employability and employability assets were discussed and the importance of critical thinking in the workplace in order to develop service through decision-making, problem-solving and the application of leadership skills was appraised. Professional practice was also discussed in relation to postgraduate skills, and then the current context of health and social care was introduced in relation to the emerging patient-led and consumerist ideology. Finally, the reader was invited to consider how Master's level skills can be applied in order to improve the student's 'employability'.

Reflection	
Identify at least three things that you have learned from this chapter.	1. 2. 3.
How do you plan to use this knowledge?	1. 2. 3.
How will you evaluate the effectiveness of your plan?	1. 2. 3.
What further knowledge and evidence do you need?	1. 2. 3.

FURTHER READING

NHS Institute for Innovation and Improvement (2007a) *Improvement Leaders' Guides.* Warwick: NHSI

These excellent user-friendly guides give an outstanding overview of the essential elements of leading improvement in the National Health Service but the principles are universal and can be applied across all health and social care settings. They can be found at **www.institute. nhs.uk/improvementleadersguides**

REFERENCES

Alfaro-LeFevre, R. (1995) *Critical Thinking in Nursing: A Practical Approach*. Philadelphia: Saunders

Alimo-Metcalfe, B. (2003) 'Stamp of greatness'. *Health Services Journal*, 26 June: 28–32

American Association of Colleges of Nurses (1996) *The Essentials of Master's Education or Advanced Practice Nursing*. **www.aacn.nche.edu/Education/pdf/MasEssentials96.pdf** (last accessed 15 January 2013)

Ashby, C. (2006) 'Models for reflective practice'. *Practice Nurse*, 32(10): 28–32

Atherton, J.S. (2009) 'Learning and teaching; deep and surface learning (On-line) UK'. **www.learningandteaching.info/learning/deepsurf.htm** (last accessed 15 January 2013)

Atherton, J.S. (2010) 'Writing at Master's level (On-line) UK'. **www.doceo.co.uk/academic/m_writing.htm** (last accessed 15 January 2013)

Aveyard, H. (2009) *Doing a Literature Review in Health and Social Care: A Practical Guide*. Maidenhead: McGraw-Hill

Bahr, A.H. and Zemon, M. (2000) 'Collaborative authorship in the journal literature: perspectives for academic librarians who wish to publish'. *College and Research Libraries*, 61(5): 410–19

Baldwin, C. and Chandler, G.E. (2002) 'Improving faculty publication output: the role of the writing coach'. *Journal of Professional Nursing*, 18(1): 8–15

Bandman, E.L. and Bandman, B. (1995) *Critical Thinking in Nursing* (2nd Ed.). Norwalk: Appleton and Lange

Baume, D. (2009) *Writing and Using Good Learning Outcomes*. Leeds: Metropolitan University

Baxter Magolda, M. (1992) 'Epistemological development in graduate and professional education'. *Review of Higher Education*, 19(3): 304. Cited in Moon, J. (2008) *Critical Thinking: An Exploration of Theory and Practice*. London: Routledge

Beauchamp, T. and Childress, F. (2001) *Principles of Biomedical Ethics* (5th Ed.). Oxford: Oxford University Press

Becker, L. (2004) *How to Manage Your Postgraduate Course*. Basingstoke: Palgrave Macmillan

Belcher, W.L. (2009) *Writing Your Journal Article in 12 weeks – A Guide to Academic Publishing Success*. London: Sage

Benner, P. (1984) *From Novice to Expert Suggests: Excellence and Power in Clinical Nursing Practice*. California: Addison-Wesley

Bilton, T., Bennett, K., Jones, P., Stanworth, M., Sheard, K. and Webster, A. (2002) *Introductory Sociology* (4th Ed.). London and Basingstoke: Macmillan

Bloom, B.S. (1956) *Taxonomy of Educational Objectives: Cognitive Domain/ Affective Domain*. New York: David Mackay Company

Boice, R. and Jones, F. (1984) 'Why academics don't write'. *Journal of Higher Education*, cited in Steinert, Y. *et al.* (2008) 'Writing for publication in medical education: the benefit of faculty development work shop and peer writing group'. *Medical Teacher*, 30: 280–5

Boyd, E. and Fales, A. (1983) 'Reflective learning: the key to learning from experience'. *Journal of Humanistic Psychology*, 23(2): 99–117

Burls, A. (2009) *What is Critical Appraisal?* (2nd Ed.). Critical Appraisal Skills Programme University of Oxford

Burns, J. (1978) *Leadership*. New York: Harper

Burns, R. (1995) *The Adult Learner at Work*. Sydney: Business and Professional Publishing

Burns, T. and Sinfield, S. (2004) *Teaching, Learning and Study Skills*. London: Sage

Caldwell, T. (2008) 'Beat the Cheat Information'. *World Review*, November 2008: 13–14

Canadian Task Force on the Periodic Health Examination (1979) 'The periodic health examination'. *Canadian Medical Association Journal*, 121: 1193–254

Carper, B.A. (1978) 'Fundamental patterns of knowing in nursing'. *Advances in Nursing Science*, 1978(1): 13–23

Centre for Evidence Based Medicine (2009) *What is EBM?* **www.cebm.net** (last accessed 15 January 2013)

Chandler, D. (1995) *The Act of Writing: A Media Theory Approach*. Aberystwyth: Prifysgol Cymru

Coad, J. (2006) 'Searching for and using grey literature'. *Nursing Times*, 102 (50): 35–6

Conrad, C., Howard, J. and Miller, S. (1993) in American Association of Colleges of Nurses (1996) *The Essentials of Master's Education or Advanced Practice Nursing*. **www.aacn.nche.edu/Education/pdf/MasEssentials96.pdf** (last accessed 15 January 2013)

Cottrell, S. (2008) *The Study Skills Handbook* (3rd Ed.). Basingstoke: Palgrave Macmillan

Craswell, G. (2005) *Writing for Academic Success: A Postgraduate Guide*. London: Sage

Crinson, I. (2008) *Health Policy: A Critical Perspective*. London: Sage

Daly, W.M. (1998) 'Critical thinking as an outcome of nursing education. What visit? Why is it important to nursing practice'? *Journal of Advanced Nursing Practice*, 28(2): 232–331

Daly, W.M. (2001) 'The development of an alternative method in the assessment of critical thinking as an outcome of nurse education'. *Journal of Advanced Nursing*, 36(1): 120–30

Davenport (1993) 'Is there any way out of the andragogy mess?' in Thorpe, M., Edwards, R. and Hanson, A. (eds) *Culture and Processes of Adult Learning*. London: Routledge

Day, A. (2007) *How to Get Research Published in Journals* (2nd Ed.). London: Gower

Denby, N., Swift, H., Butroyd, R., Glazzard, J. and Price, J. (2008) *Master's Level Study in Education: A Guide to Success for PGCE Students*. Buckingham: Open University Press

Department of Health (1996) *Clinical Effectiveness Reference Pack*. London: DH

Department of Health (2001) *Working Together, Learning Together: A Framework for Lifelong Learning in the NHS*. London: DH. **http://webarchive.nationalarchives. gov.uk/+/www.dh.gov.uk/en/Publicationsandstatistics/Publications/ PublicationsPolicyAndGuidance/DH_4009558** (last accessed 31 January 2013)

Department of Health (2004) *The NHS Knowledge and Skills Framework and the Development Review Process*. London: TSO

Department of Health (2008) *NHS Next Stage Review: A High Quality Workforce*. London: DH

Department of Health (2010) *Equity and Excellence: Liberating the NHS*. London: DH. **www.dh.gov.uk/en/Publicationsandstatistics/Publications/PublicationsPolicy AndGuidance/DH_117353** (accessed 15 January 2013)

Dewey, J. (1910) *How We Think*, cited in McGregor, D. (2007) *Developing Thinking, Developing Learning: A Guide to Thinking Skills in Education*. Maidenhead: Open University Press

Driscoll, J. and Driscoll, A. (2002) 'Writing an article for publication: an open invitation'. *Journal of Orthopedic Nursing*, 6: 144–52

EBNP (Evidence Based Nursing Practice) (2013) *The Hierarchy of Evidence*. **www.ebnp. co.uk/The%20Hierarchy%20of%20Evidence.htm** (last accessed 31 January 2013)

Ennis, R. (1996) *Critical Thinking*. NJ: Prentice-Hall

Facione, N., Facione P. and Sanchez, C. (1994) 'Critical thinking disposition as a measure of competent clinical judgment: the development of the Californian critical thinking disposition inventory'. *Journal of Nursing Education*, 33(8): 345–50

Fairly, D. and Closs, S.J. (2006) 'Evaluation of a nurse consultant's clinical activities and the search for patient outcomes in critical care'. *Journal of Clinical Nursing*, 15: 1106–14

Fook, J. and Gardner, F. (2007) *Practising Critical Reflection*. Maidenhead: McGraw-Hill

Garner, M. and Wallace, C. (1997) 'Supporting Master's degree students', in Knight, P. (ed.) *Learning, Teaching and Curriculum in Taught Master's Degrees*. London: Cassell Education

Gatrell, C. (2006) *Managing Part-time Study*. Maidenhead: Open University Press

Gibbs, G. (1988) *Learning by Doing: A Guide to Teaching and Learning Methods*. Oxford: Oxford Polytechnic Further Education Unit

Giles, K. and Hedge, N. (2002) 'The manager's good study guide', in Gatrell, C. (2006) *Managing Part-time Study*. Maidenhead: Open University Press

Gimenez, J. (2007) *Writing for Nursing and Midwifery Students*. Basingstoke: Palgrave

Girot, E.A. (1995) 'Preparing the practitioner for advanced academic study: the development of critical thinking'. *Journal of Advanced Nursing*, 21: 387–94

Gopee, N. (2002) 'Human and social capital as facilitators of lifelong learning in nursing'. *Nurse Education Today*, 22: 608–16

Greenhalgh, T. (1997) 'How to read a paper: getting your bearings (deciding what the paper is about)'. *BMJ*, Jul, 315: 243–46

Harper, M.G. (2006) 'High tech cheating'. *Nurse Education Today*, 26(8): 672–79

Hartley, J. (2008) *Academic Writing and Publishing: A Practical Handbook*. London: Routledge

Harvard, L. (2007) 'How to conduct an effective and valid literature search'. *Nursing Times*, 103(45): 32–3

Hayes, S. and Llewellyn, A. (2010) *The Care Process: Assessment, Planning, Implementation and Evaluation in Health and Social Care*. Exeter: Reflect Press

Hayes, S and Mackreth, P. 'Methods of assessment', in Smith, A., McAskill, H. and Jack, K. (2009) *Developing Advanced Skills in Practice Teaching*. Basingstoke: Palgrave Macmillan

Hicks, S. (1993) 'A survey of midwives' attitudes to, and involvement in, research: the first stage in identifying needs for a staff development programme'. *Midwifery*, 9: 51–2

Higher Education Academy (2004) *Occasional Paper No. 4 The Development of Critical Reflection in the Health Professions*. London: HEA

Higher Education Funding Council (2010) *Research Excellence Framework*. **www.ref.ac.uk** (last accessed 31 January 2013)

Higher Education Policy Institute and the British Library (2010) *Postgraduate Education in the United Kingdom*. London: British Library

Hillage, J. and Pollard, E. (1998) *Employability: Developing A Framework For Policy Analysis*. Institute for Employment Studies. **www.education.gov.uk/publications/ eOrderingDownload/RB85.pdf** (last accessed 31 January 2013)

House, G. (2010) *Postgraduate Education in the United Kingdom*. London: Higher Education Policy Initiative and the British Library

International Committee of Medical Journal Editors (2009) *Uniform Requirements for Manuscripts Submitted to Biomedical Journals: Ethical Considerations in the Conduct and Reporting of Research: Authorship and Contributorship*. **www.icmje.org/ethical_1author. html** (last accessed 15 January 2013)

Jasper, M. (2006) *Professional Development, Reflection and Decision Making*. Oxford: Blackwell Publishing

Johns, C. (1995) 'Framing learning through reflection within Carper's fundamental ways of knowing'. *Journal of Advanced Nursing*, 22: 226–34

Johns, C. (1996) 'Visualising and realising caring in practice through guided reflection'. *Journal of Advanced Nursing*, 24: 1135–43

Johnson, T. (1972) *Professions and Power*. London: Macmillan

Jones, S.A. and Brown, L. (1991) 'Critical thinking: impact of nursing Education'. *Journal of Advanced Nursing*, 16(5): 529–33

Keen, A. (2007) 'Writing for publication: pressures, barriers and support strategies'. *Nurse Education Today*, 27: 382–88

Kleinpell, R.N. (2002) 'Rediscovering the value of the journal club'. *American Journal of Critical Care*, 11: 412–14

Knight P.T. (Ed.) (1997) *Learning, Teaching and Curriculum in Taught Master's Degrees*. London: Cassell

Knowles, M. (1980) *The Modern Practice of Adult Education*. Chicago: Follet

Knowles, M.S. (1990) *The Adult Learner: A Neglected Species* (4th Ed.). Houston: Gulf Publishing Company

Kotter, J. (2001) 'What leaders really do'. *Harvard Business Review*, December: 85–96

Leeds Metropolitan University (2009) *The Little Book of Essay Writing*. **http://skillsforlearning.leedsmet.ac.uk/publications/essay_writing.shtml** (last accessed 31 January 2013)

Lees, D. (2002) *Graduate Employability*. **www.qualityresearchinternational.com/esecttools/esectpubs/leeslitreview.pdf** (last accessed 31 January 2013)

Leitch, S. (2006) *Leitch Review of Skills: Prosperity for All in the Global Economy – World Class Skills*. Norwich: HMSO

Lieb, S. (1991) *Principles of Adult Learning*. **www.lindenwood.edu/education/andragogy/andragogy/2011/Lieb_1991.pdf** (last accessed 31 January 2013)

Mackintosh, C. (1998) 'Reflection: a flawed strategy for the nursing profession'. *Nurse Education Today*, 18: 553–7

Manogue, M., Kelly, M., Bartakova Masaryk, S., Brown, G., Catalanotto, F., Choo-Soo, T., Delap, E., Godoroja, P., Morio, I., Rotgans, J. and Saag, M. (2002) 'Evolving methods of assessment'. *European Journal of Dental Education*, 6, Suppl. (3): 53–66

Marquis, B. and Huston, C. (2008) *Leadership Roles and Management Functions in Nursing: Theory and Application* (6th Ed.). Philadelphia: Lippincott

Maxwell, G., Scott, B., MacFarlane, D. and Williamson, E. (2009) 'Employers as stakeholders in postgraduate employability skills development'. *International Journal of Management Education* 8(2): 1–10

McQueen, D. (2002) 'The evidence debate'. *Journal of Epidemiology Community Health*, 56: 83–4

McVeigh, H. (2008) 'Factors influencing the utilisation of e-learning in post-registration nursing students'. *Nurse Education Today*, 29: 91–9

Mintzberg, H. (1996) 'Musings on management'. *Harvard Business Review*, July–August: 74(4): 61–7

Moncur, M. (2007) *Quotations by Author*. **www.quotationspage.com/quotes/Sir_Francis_Bacon** (last accessed 15 January 2013)

Moon, J.A. (2004) *A Handbook of Reflective and Experiential Learning: Theory and Practice*. London: Routledge Falmer

Moon, J. (2008) *Critical Thinking: An Exploration of Theory and Practice*. London: Routledge

Moran, A.P.(2000) *Managing Your Own Learning at University: A Practice Guide*. Dublin: Dublin Press

Morrison, M. (2006) *SWOT Analysis*. **http://thebir.com/created/SWOTanalysis.html** (last accessed 31 January 2013)

Murray, R. (2002) 'Writing development for lecturers moving from further to higher education: a case study'. *Journal of Further and Higher Education*, 26(3): 229–39

NHS Executive (1998) *Achieving Effective Practice: A Clinical Effectiveness and Research Information Pack for Nurses, Midwives and Health Visitors*. **www.dh.gov.uk/assetRoot/04/04/24/62/04042462.pdf** (last accessed 31 January 2013)

NHS Institute for Innovation and Improvement (2007a) *Improvement Leaders' Guides*. Warwick: NHSI

NHS Institute for Innovation and Improvement (2007b) *Improvement Leaders' Guides: Redesigning Roles: Personal and Organisational Development.* Warwick: NHSI

NHS Institute for Innovation and Improvement (2007c) *Improvement Leaders' Guides: Redesigning Leading Improvement: Personal and Organisational Development.* Warwick: NHSI

Nursing and Midwifery Council (2008) *The Code: Standards of Conduct, Performance and Ethics for Nurses and Midwives.* London: NMC

O'Donnell, V., Tobbell, J., Lawthom, V. and Zammit, M. (2009) 'Transition to postgraduate study: practice, participation and the widening participation agenda'. *Active Learning in Higher Education,* 10(26)

O'Halloran, P., Porter S. and Blackwood, B. (2010) 'Evidence based practice and its critics: what is a nurse manager to do?' *Journal of Nursing Management,* 1: 90–5

Paul, R. and Elder, L. (2008) *The Miniature Guide to Critical Thinking Concepts and Tools.* Tomales, CA: Foundation for Critical Thinking Press

Petticrew, M. and Roberts, H. (2003) 'Evidence, hierarchies, and typologies: horses for courses'. *Journal of Epidemiology Community Health,* 57: 527–9

Price, B. (2004) 'Supporting nurses study: lay supporters and their work'. *Nurse Education Today,* 24: 14–19

Price, B. (2010) 'Disseminating best practice through publication in journals'. *Nursing Standard,* 24(26): 35–41

Pugsley, L. (2009) 'How to approach writing for publication in medical education'. *Education in Primary Care,* 20: 122–4

Quality Assurance Agency for Higher Education (2000) *Code of Practice – Quality and Standards in HE.* **www.qaa.ac.uk/assuringstandardsandquality/code-of-practice/Pages/default.aspx** (last accessed 31 January 2013)

Quality Assurance Agency for Higher Education (2008) *The Framework for Higher Education Qualifications in England, Wales and Northern Ireland.* **www.qaa.ac.uk/Publications/InformationAndGuidance/Documents/FHEQ08.pdf** (last accessed 31 January 2013)

Quality Assurance Agency for Higher Education (2009) *Master's Degree Characteristics (Draft for consultation).* Gloucester: QAA

Quality Assurance Agency for Higher Education (2010) *Master's Degree Characteristics.* Gloucester: QAA

Quality Assurance Agency for Higher Education (2012) *The UK Quality Code for Higher Education.* Available at: **www.qaa.ac.uk/AssuringStandardsAndQuality/quality-code/Pages/default.aspx** (last accessed 15 January 2013)

Quality Assurance Agency Scotland (2001) The Framework for Qualifications in Higher Education Institutions in Scotland (January 2001) **www.qaa.ac.uk/Publications/InformationAndGuidance/Documents/FHEQscotland.pdf** (last accessed 31 January 2013)

Quinn, F. (2000) *Principles and Practice of Nurse Education* (4th Ed.). Cheltenham: Nelson Thornes

Quinn, F. and Hughes, S. (2007) *Principles and Practice of Nurse Education*. Cheltenham: Nelson Thornes

Race, P. (2007) *How to Get a Good Degree* (2nd Ed.). Maidenhead: Open University Press

Research Councils UK (2006) **www.rcuk.ac.uk/media/news/2006news/Pages/060628. aspx** (last accessed 31 January 2013)

Richardson, J.T.E., Dawson, L., Sadlo, G., Jenkins, V. and Mcinnes, J. (2007) 'Perceived academic quality and approaches to studying in the health professions'. *Medical Teacher*, 29:108–16

Robinson, F.P. (1970) *Effective Study* (4th Ed.). New York: Harper & Row

Robinson, R., Eck, C., Keck, B and Wells, N. (2003) in Jasper, M. (2006) *Professional Development, Reflection and Decision Making*. Oxford: Blackwell Publishing

Rolfe, G. and Gardner, L. (2006) 'Do not ask who I am: confession, emancipation and self management through reflection'. *Journal of Nursing Management*, 14: 593–600

Schön, D. (1987) *The Reflective Practitioner*. San Francisco: Jossey-Bass

Shapiro, A. and the University of York (2009) *Rome Wasn't Built in a Day – The Impact of Advanced Practitioners on Service Delivery and Patient Care in Greater Manchester Final Report*. Acton: Shapiro and NHS North West

Shin, K.R., Lee, J.H., Ha, J.Y. and Kim, K.H. (2006) 'Critical thinking dispositions in baccalaureate nursing students'. *Journal of Advanced Nursing*, 56(2): 182–9

Skills for Health (2009) News Release 12 November 2009 *Skills for Health launches core standards for Assistant Practitioners*. **www.skillsforhealth.org.uk/~/media/Resource-Library/PDF/Core-standards-for-Assistant-Practitioners.ashx** (accessed 15 January 2013)

Staudt, M., Dulmus, C. and Bennett, G. (2003) 'Facilitating writing by practitioners: survey of practitioners who have published'. *Social Work*, 48(1): 75–83

Steinert, Y., Mcleod, P., Liben, S. and Snell, L. (2008) 'Writing for publication in medical education: the benefits of a faculty development workshop and peer writing group'. *Medical Teacher*, 30: 280–5

Stinson, S. (2003) 'Participation of women in human biology'. *American Journal of Human Biology*, 15: 440–5

Stuart, C. (2007) *Assessment Supervision and Support in Clinical Practice*. London: Churchill Livingstone

Taylor, B.J. (2000) *Reflective Practice: A Guide for Nurses and Midwives*. Buckingham: Open University Press

Tennant, M. (1996) *Psychology and Adult Learning*. London: Routledge

Thaiss, C. and Zawacki, T.M. (2006) *Engaged Writers, Dynamic Disciplines: Research on the Academic Writing Life*. Portsmouth, NH: Boynton/Cook, Heinemann

Thomson, A.M. (2005) 'Writing for publication in this refereed journal'. *Midwifery*, 21: 190–4

Tobbell, J., O'Donnell, V. and Zammit, M. (2008) 'Exploring practice and participation in transition to postgraduate social science study'. York: Higher Education Academy

Tobbell, J., O'Donnell, V., Lawton, R. and Zammit, M. (2009) 'Transition to postgraduate study: practice participation and the widening participation agenda'. *Active Learning in Higher Education*, 10: 26–40

Tudor Hart, J. (2006) *The Political Economy of Health Care: A Clinical Perspective*. Bristol: Policy Press

University of Worcester (2010) *Moving On: Academic Writing.* **www.worc.ac.uk/movingon/ Academic%20writing.pdf** (last accessed 15 January 2013)

Wager, E. (2005) *Getting Research Published: An A to Z of Publication Strategy*. Oxford: Radcliffe Publishing

Warn, J. and Tranter, P. (2001) 'Measuring quality in higher education: a competency approach'. *Quality in Higher Education*, 7 (3): 191–8

Wood, D. (2008) 'Problem-based learning'. *Student BMJ*, 16:183 | 17

Wood, M.J. (2009) 'The ethics of writing for publication'. *Clinical Nursing Research*, 18(3)

Yakovchuk, N. (2004) *An Analysis of On-line Student Plagiarism Prevention Guidelines at British Universities*. Warwick: University of Warwick

INDEX